Learning Disabilities

Learning Disabilities

Charles J. Golden, Lisa K. Lashley, Jared S. Link,
Matthew Zusman, Maya Pinjala,
Christopher Tirado, and Amber Deckard

MP MOMENTUM PRESS
HEALTH

MOMENTUM PRESS, LLC, NEW YORK

Learning Disabilities

First published in 2016 by
Momentum Press, LLC
222 East 46th Street, New York, NY 10017
www.momentumpress.net

ISBN-13: 978-1-60650-833-6 (paperback)
ISBN-13: 978-1-60650-834-3 (e-book)

Momentum Press Child Clinical Psychology "Nuts and Bolts" Collection

Cover and interior design by Exeter Premedia Services Private Ltd., Chennai, India

First edition: 2016

10 9 8 7 6 5 4 3 2 1

Printed in the United States of America.

Abstract

Clinicians within the fields of neuropsychology and school psychology may find this text to be a useful guide in understanding and assessing the disparate learning disorders. This resource reviews the extant literature regarding the current status of diagnosis, conceptualization, and evaluative methods of reading, mathematics, writing, and nonverbal learning disorders. Interventions will be elucidated regarding the remediation of the various subtypes of learning disorders. This book is specifically tailored to aid busy clinicians and students-in-training in accruing the clinical acumen pertinent to the assessment of learning disorders. Case studies are included that will give insight into the types of cases and profiles clinicians will often come across in practice.

Keywords

disorder of written expression, evaluation and assessment of learning disorder, learning disorder, learning disorder diagnosis, math disorder, neuropsychological assessment of learning disorder, nonverbal learning disorder, reading disorder, specific learning disorder

Contents

CHAPTER 1

Description and Diagnosis

With the passing of the *Education for All Handicapped Children Act*, now called the *Individuals with Disabilities Education Act 2004* (*IDEA*), by Congress in 1975, those experiencing trouble in various skills necessary for academic success were finally provided with the opportunity to receive free appropriate public education (Cortiella and Horowitz 2014). This landmark civil rights measure has been amended several times since 1975 to include various types of disabilities that have shown to hinder an individual's ability to perform successfully in schools, colleges, and workplaces. The nosology of a learning disability (LD) has changed with the federal special education law and includes a wide variety of disabilities that can affect one's learning abilities such as brain injury, mathematics disorder, reading disorder, attention-deficit/hyperactivity disorder (ADHD), disorder of written expression, emotional disorders, visual processing disorder, auditory processing disorder, nonverbal learning disabilities, and many others (Cortiella and Horowitz 2014). Once individuals have been identified as having a disability that affects their performance in schools, colleges, or the workplace, accommodations can be made to help them succeed.

Prevalence rates of LDs have varied depending on the definition and method of which cases are verified. Current rates estimate that approximately 5 percent of American public school students have been classified as having an LD as defined under IDEA. The lifetime prevalence of LDs in children in the United States has been estimated to be 9.7 percent, and has been shown to have a higher prevalence in those with special health care needs (27.8 percent; Altarac and Saroha 2007). According to the National Center for Learning Disabilities (Cortiella and Horowitz 2014), approximately 19 percent of those diagnosed with an LD drop out of school, and Blacks, Hispanics, and males are over-represented in the LD category. In addition, it has been reported that there is a higher incidence of LDs in children and adolescents that are at an economic disadvantage, suffer comorbid psychiatric and health-related conditions, and live in foster care, according to investigations carried out by the National Council on Disability.

Currently, IDEA utilizes the term "specific learning disability (SLD)" and defines this as

> a disorder in one or more of the basic psychological processes involved in understanding or in using language, spoken or written, which disorder may manifest itself in the imperfect ability to listen, think, speak, read, write, spell, or do mathematical calculations. Such term includes such conditions as perceptual disabilities, brain injury, minimal brain dysfunction, dyslexia, and developmental aphasia. Such term does not include a learning problem that is primarily the result of visual, hearing or motor abilities, of mental retardation, of emotional disturbance, or of environmental, cultural, or economic disadvantage. (20 U.S.C. § 1401)

Similar definitions have been described in the Diagnostic and Statistical Manual of Mental Disorders, Fourth Edition, Text Revised (DSM-IV-TR; APA [American Psychiatric Association] 2000), and the recently released Diagnostic and Statistical Manual of Mental Disorders, Fifth Edition (DSM-5; APA 2013). Each of these definitions have differences as well as similarities, and given that many institutions have not officially adopted the DSM-5, both will be discussed below.

The DSM-IV-TR defines LDs as occurring when achievement level on standardized tests in reading, mathematics, or written expression is *significantly* below that which is expected given an individual's age, education level, and measured intelligence. This distinction is made via a discrepancy-based model in which there must be *at least* a standard deviation difference of 1.5 to 2 between the achievement level in a particular area and their overall IQ (APA 2000). The DSM-IV-TR utilizes different methods of classifying specific learning difficulties through distinctive criteria that must be met in order for a diagnosis of an LD to be made. These particular diagnoses include: reading disorder, mathematics disorder, and disorder of written expression.

Reading Disorder

According to the DSM-IV-TR (APA 2000), the incidence rate of reading disorder is difficult to determine due to lack of separation of other LDs. Despite this, it has been estimated that the rate of reading disorder is approximately 7 percent in school-aged children (Moll et al. 2014). A typical presentation of reading disorder is frequently not discovered until first grade or second grade, as formal reading instruction does not typically begin until that time. In more severe cases, the child may present with difficulties much earlier and is frequently accompanied with comorbid diagnoses such as speech sound disorder and even ADHD (Pennington 2006). While previous estimates of gender differences have described males as being more likely to be diagnosed with a reading disorder (60 to 80 percent; APA 2000), more recent estimates have not found significant gender differences (Moll et al. 2014). The reason for the prior differences is likely due to the lack of consensus on appropriate discrepancy models and separation of comorbid LDs. While some investigators have recently suggested a lack of gender differences, others have indicated that males are more likely to be referred for evaluation due to their propensity to engage in disruptive behaviors and expression of frustration associated with reading difficulties (Quinn and Wagner 2013). The DSM-IV criteria for reading disorder include: (1) Reading achievement, as measured by individually administered standardized tests of reading accuracy or comprehension, is substantially below their expected level, based on the person's chronological age, measured intelligence, and age-appropriate education; (2) the disturbance above significantly interferes with academic achievement or activities of daily living that require reading skills; and (3) if a sensory deficit is present, the reading difficulties are in excess of those usually associated with it. If a sensory deficit is the sole cause of the problem, that would be the appropriate diagnosis.

Mathematics Disorder

The prevalence rate of mathematics disorder or developmental dyscalculia has been estimated to be in the approximate range of 3 to 6.5 percent in a variety of countries including the United States, Germany, India, and Israel (Badian 1983; Lewis, Hitch, and Walker 1994; Gross-Tsur,

Manor, and Shalev 1996; Hein, Bzufka, and Neumärker 2000; Ramaa and Gowramma 2002; Shalev 2004). This rate differs in comparison to the DSM-IV-TR, which estimates the prevalence to be approximately 1 percent in school-aged children (APA 2000). A common problem seen when evaluating a mathematics disorder is the incidence of mathematical anxiety, which can serve as a major influence in problems described and seen by clinicians. These individuals tend to emphasize speed over accuracy, which can cause them to perform poorly on even basic mathematical problems (Shalev 2004). Such psychological factors can contribute to poor performance in school and can even lead to misdiagnosis.

Recent estimates have indicated that the rate of mathematics disorder diagnosis is approximately similar between genders (Shalev 2004). In contrast, significant differences have been shown in the direction of males in a subclinical population (Moll et al. 2014). Devine et al. (2013) argue that gender differences are dependent on the model used when making a diagnosis of mathematics disorder. When using absolute values (i.e., 1 to 1.5 SD), no gender differences are seen; however, when using mathematics to reading discrepancy, females are more likely to meet criteria for a mathematics disorder (Devine et al. 2013).

DSM-IV-TR criteria for mathematics disorder include: (1) Mathematics achievement in the area of mathematics on standardized tests, and is deemed to be significantly below what would be expected for the individual's age, intelligence, and education level using a criteria of a 1.5 standard deviation impairment when compared to expected levels. (2) The problems include such issues as difficulties in writing or printing numbers, counting, adding and subtracting, working with mathematical signs, or learning names that include numbers. (3) Problems also include difficulties in performing calculations, comprehending word problems, and an inability to grasp mathematical information. (4) Other impairments may be seen in various areas including "linguistic" skills (e.g., understanding or naming mathematical terms, operations, or concepts), "perceptual" skills (e.g., recognizing or reading numerical symbols or arithmetic signs, and clustering objects into groups), "attention" skills (e.g., copying numbers or figures correctly, remembering to add in "carried" numbers, and observing operational signs), and "mathematical" skills (e.g., following sequences of mathematical steps, counting objects, and learning multiplication tables). Furthermore, this deficit must inter-fere with their academic achievement and/or other activities that involve the need or use of mathematical ability (e.g., calculating change or tip, creating a budget, paying taxes, etc.). (5) The mathematics problem must significantly interfere with academic achievement or activities that require mathematical ability (such as measuring or calculations in the workplace. (6) If a sensory deficit is present, the problems must exceed those expected by that deficit (e.g., a blind person would not be expected to read printed mathematical symptoms). If a sensory deficit is the complete cause of the problem, that deficit (e.g., blindness) is the proper diagnosis.

Disorder of Written Expression

Writing is a skill that is considered one of the most complex abilities humans learn, and is crucial for academic success (Katusic et al. 2009). According to the DSM-IV-TR, prevalence rates for disorders of written expression (DWE) are difficult to determine given the lack of concern for separating the LDs, and is rare being diagnosed without other LDs (APA 2000). In contrast, Katusic et al. (2009) suggest an incidence rate of 6.9 to 14.7 percent, and is frequently found among males than females. This indicates that DWE is approximately similar in prevalence as reading disorder.

Key characteristics of DWE involve a general difficulty with writing that may be associated with an overall inability to organize one's thoughts onto paper, which can be inarticulate and lacking in comprehensiveness and understanding. Moreover, the diagnosis is generally a combination of difficulties in the individual's ability to compose written texts evidenced by grammatical or punctuation errors within sentences, poor paragraph organization, multiple spelling errors, and excessively poor handwriting. The individual's poor handwriting includes letters of the alphabet that are reversed, letters of the alphabet that are rotated, letters of the alpha-bet that are unrecognizable, and random mixture of cursive and printed letters. An additional characteristic of many individuals with DWE is an awkward grip of a pencil or pen, which likely contributes to the poor handwriting that has been observed; however, this needs to be delineated from a fine motor delay.

For a diagnosis of DWE to be made, according to the DSM-IV-TR, an individual's writing ability as measured by standardized neuropsychological tests must be substantially below (1.5+ SDs) her or his chronological age, measured intellectual abilities, and education. In addition, the reported and measured difficulty must interfere with her or his academic achievements or activities in daily life, which requires the ability to write or organize her or his thoughts in written format. If a fine motor delay or other sensory or motor problem exists, the clinician must take into account these factors, and the writing ability must be in excess of what would typically be associated with these disorders (i.e., over and above legibility of handwriting). In these instances, it is important for clinicians to consider the quality of what is written in the evaluation rather than how it is written. For example, an individual with a fine motor delay may perform poorly on timed written tasks, but does well on measures that assess how well one can compose short sentences (i.e., focus is on syntax, grammar, punctuation, and flow).

Complete diagnostic criteria from DSM-IV-TR for DWE include: (1) Writing ability as measured by standardized tests of functional assessments of actual writing samples are considerably (using 1.5 standard deviations) below the individual's expected level based on their age, intelligence, and education; (2) the problem interferes with academic achievement or activities of daily living that require the composition of written texts (e.g., completing school assignments properly or completing memos or notes required at work in a proper manner); and (3) as with the other disorders, if the disorder is due fully to a sensory or motor deficit, that would be the appropriate diagnosis. For example, a paralyzed individual unable to move her or his hands would not be expected to be able to physically write letters.

Nonverbal Learning Disorder

The least recognized and discussed LD, nonverbal learning disorder (NVLD) could likely be confused as Asperger's disorder, now subsumed under autistic spectrum disorder in DSM-5, due to the presentation of symptoms and can even occur comorbidly with autistic disorder (Roman 1998). Those with NVLD are highly verbal, but struggle with understanding the big picture of social and academic settings, have difficulty with problem solving and performing math computations that are not overlearned, and do poorly on visuospatial and motor tasks (Cortiella and Horowitz 2014). Individuals with NVLD evidence intact verbal skills, verbal expression, auditory attention, but may be less likely to explore their environment or even show interest in others or social situations (Rourke 1995).

NVLD has been previously described as being characterized by three cardinal areas of dysfunction, including visual and tactile problems, psychomotor coordination, and forming new concepts or understanding novel information (Rourke 1995; Dhanalakshmi 2015). Furthermore, it is likely that those with NVLD struggle with perceptual reasoning abilities such as is required on the Wechsler Intelligence Scales including: analysis and synthesis of visual information, the use of non-verbal abstract reasoning, and to perceive and organize visual information. A clinical profile of a child or adult would experience a significant discrepancy between her or his verbal skills and nonverbal abilities with overall verbal scores being significantly higher than nonverbal. More specifically, Rourke and Tsatsanis (2000) described that those with NVLD have trouble appreciating the nonverbal aspects of communication, and often experience problems with prosody, tone of voice, and understanding sarcasm. Furthermore, these authors elaborated on additional clinical characteristics of NVLD including: poor complex psychomotor skills typically affecting the left side of the body, trouble with time estimation, excellent rote verbal memory skills, increased dependence on language abilities to relate interpersonally, gather information, mechanical arithmetic deficits, and evidence poor social judgment, and can be seen as hyperactive in early school years.

Rourke and Tsatsanis (2000) describe a conceptual framework that helps elucidate the clinical manifestations of NVLD in terms of interplay between primary, secondary, tertiary, and linguistic neuropsychological strengths and weaknesses. In other words, this model takes into account the belief that elementary deficits influence higher order impairment. Rourke and Tsatsanis (2000)'s model of NVLD posits that there is a natural flow of deficits starting with primary problems including deficits in tactile and visual perception and understanding, lack of complex psychomotor abilities, and inability to integrate novel information. This is hypothesized to further influence problems with tactile attention, visual attention, and adaptive skills associated with exploratory behaviors. From this, higher cognitive dysfunction or tertiary neuropsychological deficits can be seen in the form of tactile memory, visual memory, concept formation, and problem solving. This further exacerbates verbal functions including oral motor praxis, prosody, understanding semantic content, and pragmatics.

The lack of attention and current research into this disorder has resulted in no diagnostic category that is recognized by the DSM-IV-TR or DSM-5. This is likely due to a number of reasons including: (1) difficulty in differentiating between NVLD and high functioning autism or Asperger's disorder due to similar symptom presentations regarding social ineptitude and lack of approach behaviors toward their environment; and (2) these individuals often have strong verbal skills, rote verbal memory, phonology, and auditory and verbal attention skills; therefore, they may be less recognized as having a serious problem by those who know them such as their parents, siblings, or teachers. As a result of an appropriate DSM diagnosis for NVLD, those that express characteristics of this disorder would likely be diagnosed with Learning Disorder Not Otherwise Specified as per the DSM-IV-TR.

Despite this, distinctions between the two disorders should be made. One major difference between NVLD and Asperger's disorder is theory of mind, which has been described as an ability to recognize that everyone has her or his own thoughts and beliefs that can be drastically different from our own (Goldman et al. 2012). A major feature of Asperger's disorder is the absence of such a cognitive capacity, which makes these disorders distinctly different from NVLD. In NVLD, the ability to recognize these differences is relatively intact. Furthermore, another cardinal feature is the tendency to have extremely rigid and inflexible interests and behaviors in Asperger's disorder, whereas NVLD typically does experience such issues. Emotionally speaking, those with NVLD experience a range of normal emotions, but are deficient in the expression and recognition of these feelings in others, whereas those with Asperger's disorder do not experience normal emotions as well as others do and have difficulty understanding these feelings (Rourke and Tsatsanis 1996; Rourke and Tsatsanis 2000; Rourke 2005).

It should also be noted that in the absence of any approved definition of NVLD, many other definitions may be involved. For example, one version of NVLD may affect only the appreciation of spatial relationships so that all other skills and abilities are intact. In this situation, verbal learning is intact or even strong as may be all basic skills, but such heavily spatial skills in such areas as advanced mathematics, engineering, organic chemistry, architecture may be impaired, especially when three-dimensional analysis are required. This is seen as a serious disorder in individuals in undergraduate and graduate schools who have high intelligence but cannot learn things such as the spatial orientation of atoms within a complex molecule, the three-dimensional orientation of the anatomy of the brain and body, or an appreciation of the three-dimensional aspects of a building or bridge.

In more serious cases, NVLD may involve impairment in the processing of more fundamental factors such as nonverbal analysis of one's emotions, body language, and the emotions of others. In such cases, there can be a substantial overlap with the symptoms of Asperger's, although Asperger's clients may not have an inability to perceive the type of spatial relationships discussed above but may share the emotional analyses issues. It is clearly not the case that every person with Asperger's has NVLD and vice versa (Ozonoff and McMahon-Griffith 2000). While these disorders exhibit similar profiles, they are distinctly different than those with Asperger's disorder; those with NVLD have less social impairment (Klin and Volkmar 2000), experience better eye-to-eye gaze (Rourke and Tsatsanis 2000), and better theory of mind (Ozonoff and McMahon-Griffith 2000).

It is important to note that these issues are less important than they seem. While it is recognized that such diagnostic distinctions may be important to the government and bureaucracies in general for classification and eligibility for specific programs, these distinctions ignore the issue that the deficits within each specific area are on a continuum and that the severity of each underlying symptom discussed here will differ within and between individuals so that any classification is itself potentially misleading. The goal of individual diagnosis should not be classification but rather understanding of the individual as a unique person. While the medical model of classification of each person may make sense when there is a clear difference in the treatment for disorders with different diagnoses, it makes less sense in psychology and education where a "one size fits all" prescription for treating a "disorder" is highly questionable. It should also be noted that such an approach is not always appropriate in medicine as well, where it has been recognized, for example, that individuals with different genetic makeups need different treatments for what appears to be the same exact disorder. When dealing with behavioral and learning problems, the need for individualized treatment far outweighs the client's need for a specific, yet misleading, diagnostic criteria. Our focus needs to be on the person not the diagnosis.

Even still, some investigators have attempted to describe guidelines in helping clinicians to understand NVLD (Drummond, Ahmad, and Rourke 2005). Through empirical inquiry, these authors sought to develop rules for clinicians to utilize in helping to classify NVLD and basic phonological processing disability (BPPD). The authors assessed neuropsychological profiles of 124 participants aged 7 and 8 years from an archival database in order to develop the particular guidelines for diagnosing NVLD and BPPD (for specific criteria, see Drummond, Ahmad, and Rourke 2005). In order to determine specific rules for classification, the authors examined different categories of functioning including: academic achievement, motor or psychomotor, tactile or perceptual, visuospatial, auditory or perceptual, language, and problem solving. Results from their analyses revealed several key rules that were helpful in classifying definite NVLD. These rules included: (1) Memory for visual sequence is impaired by at least 1 standard deviation (measured via the Target Test; Reitan and Davison 1974). (2) Approximately two of the Wechsler Intelligence Scale for Children-Revised (WISC-R Block Design, Object Assembly, and Coding subtests) are the lowest for the Perceptual Reasoning Index. (3) Approximately two WISC-R Verbal subtests such as vocabulary, similarities, and information are the highest on that scale. (4) Tactual Performance Test times (i.e., right, left, and both hands) become increasingly worse. (5) Grip strength is approximately 1 standard deviation of the average and Grooved Pegboard Test is greater than 1 standard deviation *below* the mean. (6) WISC-R VIQ > PIQ by a minimum of 10 points. (7) Wide Range Achievement Test (WRAT; Wilkinson and Robertson 2006) reading standard scores are at least 8 points above arithmetic scores. While these rules seem promising in resolving this nosological problem revolving around NVLD, these guidelines were established using a sample of 7- to 8-year-olds with a sample size of 10; therefore, generalizability is limited. In addition, they were limited to one site and one perspective. While such attempts are admirable in that the development of set and accurate criteria would be absolutely a boon to schools, employers, and diagnosticians, the reality is that none of these attempts have been well or generally accepted and are best considered interesting rather than definitive.

DSM-5: Specific Learning Disorder

Clinicians have needed to adapt to recent categorical, dimensional, and criteria changes with the advent of the DSM-5 (APA 2013). Under the category of neurodevelopmental disorders, specific learning disorder (SLD) has subsumed all previous LDs described in DSM-IV-TR, and authors of the DSM have attempted to broaden the diagnostic category in order to reflect the scope of learning problems that have been described in recent literature. In addition, by broadening the definition and forming each of the LDs into one overarching category, clinicians will likely experience fewer challenges related to defining a specific LD from variable test scores or subclinical scores and decrease the number of affected cases that go unidentified (Tannock 2014). Moreover, the DSM-5 pushes clinicians to abandon the IQ-achievement model and cognitive processing deficits that have spanned previous DSM editions (APA 2013; Tannock 2014).

The DSM-5 (APA 2013) describes SLD as a disorder that is frequently made aware during elementary school at which time children are developing these respective skills. Deficits are often brought to the parent's attention through concerns of the child's teachers whether in the form that she or he is struggling to understand basic concepts or being behind the pace of her or his peers to learn material. Failure to establish that she or he is experiencing difficulty in a particular subject area whether it is reading, writing, or arithmetic sets the stage for additional problems later on. This is particularly problematic when the issues are mild in severity in which case difficulties may go undiagnosed for an extended period of time, which limits the child's capacity to obtain appropriate resources.

While it is not limited to a lack of diagnosis, symptoms of SLD can show heterotypic continuity in that, for example, preschool children with reading difficulties may present with trouble learning rhyming schemes and recognizing letters, even in their own name. As they progress through school, they may experience trouble writing their name, use inverted spelling, and have difficulty breaking spoken words down into multiple syllables (e.g., "racecar" into "race" and "car"). They may even struggle with recognizing phonemes of words (e.g., unable to pick the word which starts with the same sound as "bad" from a set of words such as "bat, man, dog"). In primary school, children may have difficulty with decoding words and make frequent reading errors that are suggestive of misinterpreting sounds and letters (e.g., "big" for "got"). Further, older children may struggle with proper pronunciation of multisyllable words such as "continus" instead of "continuous" or even mispronounce words due to difficulty in discriminating similar letters, for example, when a child says "aminal" instead of "animal."

Later in adolescence or even adulthood, these individuals may simply avoid tasks that involve comprehension of written material or reading aloud. Further, they may develop low self-esteem, hopelessness, anxiety, depression, and may even be criticized by parents or peers due to their difficulties. More often than not, the developing child will start to engage in internalizing or externalizing behaviors, which are frequent complaints of parents and teachers and serve as a focus of seeking an evaluation. A weary clinician should consider how these factors have been influenced and maintained by a possible SLD along with other factors including comorbidities such as ADHD, mood disorders, anxiety disorders, communication disorders, autism spectrum disorder, or other disorders that could be impacting the individual emotionally. This is when a thorough record review becomes incredibly important, as those with anxiety or depressive symptoms can give the appearance of an SLD. In the vast majority of cases such as this, these individuals will have performed roughly at or above normal level prior to the onset of the symptoms.

When attempting to diagnose SLD, clinicians need to consider the type of learning or academic difficulties the potential client is reporting.

These symptoms must have persisted for *at least* 6 months regardless of the success of any clinical interventions that have been put in place to alleviate any struggles experienced. Given that the individual LDs from DSM-IV-TR have been subsumed under the new diagnostic criteria in DSM-5, one can suffer from a variety of symptoms that are associated with a specific learning problem including, but not limited to: (1) difficulty with reading fluency, understanding words, sounding out words; (2) comprehension of simple or complex narratives or recognizing relationships and general sequences within a story; (3) trouble spelling and understanding special spelling rules (e.g., "i" before "e," except after "c" or silent letters as in "knot"); (4) inability to structure grammatically appropriate sentences, organizing paragraphs in a coherent manner, or lack of skill at conveying their thoughts onto paper; (5) trouble understanding numbers and numerical concepts and relationships, which influences them to use certain strategies such as using their fingers to help them count or talking through the problem; and (6) struggle with mathematical reasoning abilities such as applying rules or principles to solve problems.

These academic difficulties extend above and beyond the individual's intellectual ability, age, and level of education, and cause significant impairment within the academic or occupational settings. Furthermore, these learning challenges tend to be more apparent when they are asked to do tasks which are too difficult for them, such as when they are required to write lengthy or complex narratives within a certain time period or required to take timed tests. Finally, the reported academic difficulties should not be better accounted for by intellectual disabilities, uncorrected vision or hearing, other mental disorders such as depression or anxiety, neurological or cognitive disorder, poor language acquisition such as is the case with those that recently immigrated, or due to a general lack of educational attainment.

Thus, while the 1.5 standard deviation criteria is no longer required, it is clear that there must be a discrepancy from expected levels of performance based on the same intellectual and expected level of performance. This allows clinicians more flexibility in making the diagnosis than the previous criteria allowed (although many tried to circumvent these limitations in a variety of ways so that the new model better reflects the reality of what is seen in daily life).

Once it has been determined that the individual likely experiences an SLD, clinicians must identify which SLD is primarily the root of the academic issues, which includes impairment in reading, writing, and mathematics. Moreover, level of severity should also be determined (e.g., mild, moderate, or severe) in order to establish appropriate recommendations and interventions that would likely prove to be beneficial. The disorders included as subtypes are very similar to the diagnostic systems that previously existed. All of the subtypes require that the problem must have persisted for at least 6 months despite providing interventions designed to alleviate the problem. Thus, if a child has a reading problem, there should be some attempt to tutor the child or use alternate teaching techniques to address the problem before we jump to the conclusion that it is a disorder. It should also be noted that we recognize whether the problem is unusual from a developmental standpoint. For example, 5-year-olds who learn to write early often reverse letters spatially when writing. This is common in 5-year-olds (no matter how smart they may be) and should not be signs of a disorder. On the other hand, if the problem persists to the age of 7 or 8 years, the problem clearly differs from just a developmental phase.

Another related issue is not to confuse parental or educational goals with disorders. As schools have increased pressure to show high performance to gain funding or just to gain accolades, educational goals have been moved up such that skills learned previously in the first or second grade are expected of kindergarten children. Thus, in our practice, we frequently get referrals from high performance schools of children who perform on standardized tests at average or above average levels and whose work samples are completely consistent with the child's developmental level. Yet, the school wishes the child to be classified as having a disorder because they do not meet their accelerated criteria. In a school with age-appropriate expectations, such children would not be referred or perceived to have problems.

Once it is established that there is an age or intellectual appropriate problem that persists for more than 6 months, the problems need to be subclassified into specific areas that are similar to the areas of dysfunction present in earlier systems. These areas can include:

1. Poor reading skills, which may be reflected in inaccurate or slow word reading problems, such as an inability to read single words aloud

incorrectly or slowly and hesitantly, inability to recognize or identify specific letters, problems in reading sentences, guessing rather than decoding words phonetically, and difficulty sounding out words.

2. Difficulty in comprehension even when able to read or identify single words or sentences. Such individuals will read the text relatively accurately but will fail to understand or explain the meaning of what is read at a developmentally and intellectually appropriate level. This can range from a concrete understanding of what is read in younger children to the understanding of the sequence, relationships, inferences, or deeper meanings of what is read in adolescents and adults.

3. Difficulties with spelling when attempts have been made to have the child learn the spelling. Potential problems should be differentiated between children whose spelling is phonetically reasonable but incorrect because many words are not spelled as they sound in English, from more severe disorders in which the spelling is phonetically random or nonsensical or in which the individual omits letters or adds irrelevant letters. One should also not overdiagnose misspellings that come with regional pronunciations of certain words; regional pronunciation of words may insert or delete specific consonants and vowels. In such cases, the spelling is consistent with the pronunciation and thus phonetically correct although not consistent with the dictionary. In addition, some apparent spelling problems largely reflect lack of practice or effort to learn a specific spelling, which may occur when schools or parents do not place an emphasis on such practice. These are interesting problems in that they follow an individual as they grow up, so that when they enter an environment where accuracy is demanded they are not prepared (such as college or graduate school). Such problems may also arise from consistent reliance on spelling checkers rather than spelling abilities. The senior author has found that his spelling has declined as he has become more reliant on the computer to spell for him.

4. Difficulties with written expression can range from the simple ability to match a sound one hears to a written letter (writing "n" when one hers the "muh" sound), the inability to write letters to dictation or the motor inability to write the letter one intends to write to excessive grammatical or punctuation errors within sentences, employing poor paragraph organization, and the inability to clearly express basic

ideas. In young children, motor developmental issues should not be mistaken for writing disorders. Thus, familiarity with appropriate motor skills in young children is essential in evaluating the young child. As noted earlier, the trend of schools to demand these skills at earlier ages can make it look like such problems are increasing, when in fact it is the unreasonable expectation that is the problem, not the child's performance.

5. Basic mathematical problems include recognizing numbers, writing numbers, understanding the meaning of numbers, inability to count properly, inability to understand more complex numbers such as the meaning of double and triple digit numbers, difficulties mastering number sense, number facts, addition, multiplication, subtraction or division, poor understanding of numbers, their magnitude, and relationships; counting on fingers to add single-digit numbers, inability to follow through on complex calculations (such as 5×13), and getting lost in the midst of arithmetic computation and switching procedures (e.g., switching from more complex multiplication to less complex addition). Less often talked about in the literature but equally important are deficits in higher mathematical consents ranging from algebra, geometry, and trigonometry to advanced calculus and other higher level skills. These latter problems are especially important in individuals who have normal or better intelligence and normal foundational mathematical skills, but who are unable to do math at an intellectually appropriate level in high school and college. This may suggest a disorder in understanding the spatial nature of the more advanced mathematical approaches or may reflect deficits in high level verbal reasoning and logical skills. These disorders are often missed in early grades when these skills are not demanded. Difficulties with mathematical reasoning (e.g., severe difficulty applying mathematical concepts, facts, or procedures to solve quantitative problems). This often is as much a verbal processing problem as it is a mathematical issue. It is important to separate out this distinction in planning appropriate interventions or accommodations.

It is important to recognize that the specific diagnose of learning disorder Not Otherwise Specified (NOS) in DSM-IV is not present in

DSM-5. Thus unusual presentations or the use of an NVLD is not possible under the new system. However, in all of those cases, the disorder has an impact on one of the specific areas delineated above. If the disorder does not affect any of these areas, then it would not appropriately be diagnosed as SLD but diagnosed elsewhere.

In any area where an academic issue is identified, the skill must be measurably below the level expected based on the individual's chronological age. It must cause significant problems either at school or at work in tasks the individual would otherwise be expected to be able to do. They may also cause problems with other activities of daily living. These issues are generally confirmed by individually administered standardized achievement and performance measures, or by comprehensive evaluations of actual performance. After the age of 16, a documented history of leaning difficulties may be substituted for a standardized assessment. This requirement is based on the assumption that SLD is a lifetime disorder, so once clearly diagnosed and not a product of developmental inconsistencies, the disorder is generally acknowledged to be permanent. However, many agencies, schools, boards, and employers will require an updated assessment rather than relying on such a history. This use of a history alone in such cases cannot be imposed on such agencies or persons at the present time.

DSM-5 expects that learning difficulties begin during school-age years but may not become fully manifested until the demands for those affected academic skills exceed the individual's limited capabilities. This latter exception is an especially serious issue for college students, graduate students, and employees in working settings. Many milder disorders will not be evident in primary or secondary schools until the level of the task increases to a specific level. For example, the senior author was once a mathematics major who sailed through courses until third semester advanced calculus when his inability to perceive three- and n-dimensional equations within his head led to a significant impairment in processing and understanding the concepts demanded. This may show up as well in high stakes timed tests (such as SAT, ACT, GRE, LSAT, MCAT, etc.), reading or writing lengthy complex reports for a tight deadline, and excessively heavy academic loads. For example, some graduate students faced with writing diagnostic reports under a deadline find that their limitations in writing interfere with their ability to get the task done within expected time limits. In dealing with agencies and employers, many are skeptical of disorders that do not have a clear history so it becomes incumbent on the clinician to clearly explain and document why there is no evident history.

As in the previous diagnostic systems, learning difficulties cannot be better explained by intellectual disabilities, uncorrected visual or auditory acuity, other mental or neurological disorders, psychosocial adversity, lack of proficiency in the language of academic instruction, or inadequate educational instruction. This is not to suggest that such individuals do not need accommodations or special help and interventions in order to perform at their maximal levels, but such assistance would be provided under a different category. Unfortunately for individuals with an inadequate educational experience or lack of language skills, there is no legislative or other commitment to help such individuals outside of the standard school environment.

The numeric nomenclature of DSM-5 requires the general diagnosis with qualifiers to specify the exact disorder. For all of these disorders, one has a basic DSM-5 code (e.g., 315.00) with additional specifiers. The four diagnostic criteria are to be met based on a clinical synthesis of the individual's history (developmental, medical, family, and educational), school reports, and psychoeducational assessment.

For reading disorders, the DSM-5 code is 315.00; for International Classification of Disorders, Version 10 (ICD-10) it is F81.0 (with impairment in reading). These diagnosis may be qualified by adding additional descriptors including word reading accuracy, reading rate or fluency, or reading comprehension. More than one of these qualifiers may be added as appropriate. For written expression, the basic category is 315.2. Additional descriptors may be added to this diagnosis including spelling accuracy, grammar and punctuation accuracy, and clarity or organization of written expression. For mathematics, the basic code is 315.1 with impairment in mathematics. Additional descriptors may include number sense, memorization of arithmetic facts, accurate or fluent calculation, and accurate math reasoning.

Each of the disorders is also classified as current severity. Mild severity reflects difficulties in learning skills in one or two academic domains, but mild enough so they can function with appropriate accommodations or support services, especially during the school years. Moderate severity implies marked difficulties in learning skills in one or more academic domains, such that the individual requires intensive and specialized teaching during the school years. Some accommodations or supportive services at least part of the day at school, in the workplace, or at home may be needed. Severe impairment reflects substantial difficulties in multiple academic domains, which require ongoing intensive individualized and specialized teaching for most of the school years. Even with an array of appropriate accommodations or services at home, at school, or in the workplace, the individual may not be able to complete all activities efficiently.

International Classification of Disease

International Classification of Disease (ICD-10) is important as a diagnostic system because it has become the required system in medical settings and those who deal with insurance. ICD-10 uses similar categories but a different numbering system and different definitions. DSM-5 315.0 (with reading disorder) becomes F81.0. Specific criteria are either a 2 standard deviation difference between the predicted level of performance based on an individualized test of intelligence and age and the actual performance on individualized tests of achievement. However, the ICD-10 allows a second alternate method, which is a history of severe problems meeting this first criterion at an earlier age, plus a score on a spelling test, which is at least 2 standard deviations below the expected level based on age and intelligence.

This is a much more restrictive definition found in DSM-5 or within U.S. school settings. In addition, the diagnosis also requires that the deficit interfere with academic achievement or activities of daily living. The disorder cannot be the result of a visual or hearing disorder and there must be normal exposure to education and school experiences. Individuals with IQs below 70 are classified as having intellectual impairment rather than a learning disorder.

Code F81.1 is used for spelling disorders. This requires a score on a standardized spelling test at least 2 standard deviations below the expected score, as well as reading and arithmetic scores that are in the normal range (not exceeding 2 standard deviations below the expected score). Educational experiences must be within the normal range and the disorder must begin at the earliest stages of learning to spell. As with all of these diagnosis, the disorder must interfere with academic or daily living functions.

Arithmetic disorders get a code of F81.2 with similar criteria: arithmetic scores more than 2 standard deviations below expected scores and normal scores on reading and spelling. Arithmetic deficits must be present from the early stages of learning arithmetic. This cannot be used to diagnose problems that appear later in childhood or adolescence.

An additional category of F81.3 (mixed disorder of academic skills) can be used for individuals who meet the criteria of both arithmetic skills (F81.2) and either reading or spelling disorder. Two additional codes are poorly defined: F81.8 (other developmental disorders of scholastic skills) and F81.9 (developmental disorders of scholastic skills, unspecified). F81.8 is not defined at all, and F81.9 is to be used only rarely for cases of academic disability that do not meet the other criteria and is not caused by intellectual disability, visual acuity, or inadequate education.

There are clear differences between ICD-10 and DSM-5 requirements, such that the diagnosis would differ depending on which system was used. Many of the cases that would attain criteria for DSM-IV or DSM-5 would not meet the stricter ICD-10 standards. In such cases, one would be forced to use the F81.9 category if ICD-10 was required by an insurance company or hospital setting.

Summary

In considering a diagnosis of any LD, it is imperative that clinicians examine the onset of the specific problem, comorbidity with other Axis I disorders such as depression and anxiety, how these particular mental disorders can mimic problems typically associated with LDs, and how LDs can affect the onset of additional mental disorders. When creating hypotheses such as whether or not the client is experiencing a true LD or secondary problems as a result of another Axis I disorder, a thorough review of academic records should be conducted first. Typically, LDs are chronic and will be apparent by lower grades in the particular subject(s), lower standardized scores, and reported history of pervasive problems.

This is tricky to determine when the client is at an age where the majority of problems begin to surface such as in second and third grade. The primary reason for this is due to the lack of standing history of problems and previously poor grades and test scores. In such cases, a thorough history of the current problem with valid examples, school observation, and obtaining strong motivation and effort on neuropsychological tests becomes incredibly important and necessary.

Effort and motivation is quite possibly the most important aspect of any neuropsychological evaluation, and is essential in any evaluation of an LD. Clients are aware of their problems in a particular academic area and may experience irritability, anger, anxiety, dejection, and hopelessness as a result of having any type of task that is associated with problematic subject, including neuropsychological tests. For this reason, use of clinical skills during the evaluation becomes pertinent to obtaining scores that can be interpreted logically. Clinicians may find it useful to perform brief relaxation techniques prior to starting a dreaded task to ease any tension or anxiety and provide positive reinforcement when needed. Being able to recognize when a client is performing poorly due to learned helplessness versus doing poorly in the face of giving optimal effort can be crucial in making a proper diagnosis of LD.

CHAPTER 2

Conceptualization

Recently, considerable progress has been made in elucidating the definition of learning disabilities (LDs), although there remains an alternate conceptual approach to this diagnosis, partially because LD is defined differently across settings, in legal documents, and when different goals for identifying the disorder exist. Advances in science have resulted in a greater understanding of the etiology of LD, which is widely recognized as a neurodevelopmental disorder with associated cognitive abnormalities that manifest behaviorally. It is understood that the interaction of genetic, epigenetic, and environmental factors affects the brain's ability to perceive or process verbal or nonverbal information appropriately (American Psychiatric Association [APA] 2013). The evolution and acceptance of this concept has led to an increase in the development of educational programs aimed at supporting individuals with LD by helping them develop compensatory strategies to succeed. Despite the push for a unified diagnostic construct of LD, widely differing views still remain on how to operationalize these definitions across disciplines within psychology and across school districts and countries.

In school psychology settings, the primary purpose of LD evaluations is to determine eligibility for special education services. These determinations are typically based on criteria outlined by the school district, which are compliant with more general criteria set by the state boards of education to be consistent with federal regulations. The criteria utilized by school districts often diverge from the specific criteria set by the DSM-IV-TR or the DSM-5 (APA 2000, 2013), which are more closely followed by neuropsychologists and clinical psychologists. Differences in criteria for determining a diagnosis of LD can be a point of contention between professionals across different settings. Two primary approaches have emerged to identify and diagnose LD across settings, the problem-solving (instructional) and intra-individual (cognitive) approaches.

Problem-Solving Approach to Conceptualization

The problem-solving approach is associated with the school setting and involves identifying students with low achievement and providing them with interventions in the classroom. Tools, such as curriculum-based assessment, progress monitoring, and a response to intervention (RTI) service delivery model, are used to identify and monitor individuals with poor achievement (Fletcher 2002). This approach to identification of LD is not subtype specific, but provides early interventions to a broad group of learners who are struggling in the classroom in hopes of identifying those who require further intensive intervention. This approach is limited by the unclear definition of "low achievement" and a poor understanding of the specific predictors and causes of failure to respond to intervention (Reynolds and Shaywitz 2009). If a student fails to respond to the specialized instruction, it can be assumed that the student has a disabling condition (such as LD, attention-deficit/hyperactivity disorder [ADHD], or intellectual disability), or the instructional program was inadequate (Vaughn and Fuchs 2003). At this point, a comprehensive neuropsychological evaluation is typically recommended to determine the nature of the deficits (Hale et al. 2006).

Often the definition of poor achievement is set within the schools by the ability of the student to meet minimum standards that are generally set by state boards of education and their implementation of federal and state laws, which sets goals and requirements for achievement at each grade level. In turn, each state has implemented standards that define adequate student achievement, which may differ considerably from results of tests used in clinical psychology. In doing this, the school system has the goal, consistent with federal and state laws, that all students should reach minimum standards in reading, writing, and arithmetic so that all students are afforded an "adequate" educational experience. The emphasis in such programs is therefore focused on those students who fail to meet these standards as measured by tests designed for each school system, which measure progress on the standards. In turn, there is a secondary emphasis on students from groups (e.g., people for whom English is not their first language and certain identified minority groups) who traditionally have performed more poorly on such standards.

This approach therefore relies less on psychological and neuropsychological tests, but more on student performance. Discrepancies with IQ are not important nor often are other conditions that may cause the problem, since the focus is primarily on achievement alone. It has the advantage of extending accommodations and services to a wider group of students who would not qualify under a discrepancy approach, but it ignores disabilities in higher functioning individuals whose achievement manages to reach minimum levels.

Intra-Individual Approach to Conceptualization

The intra-individual approach to LD identification focuses primarily on assessing specific cognitive domains to provide explanations for unexpected academic underachievement through comprehensive evaluation. The key component of this approach is the idea that the unexpected poor academic performance, which is a defining feature of LD, is evidenced through a discrepancy between intact cognitive and deficient academic abilities (Kaufman 2008). Weaknesses to this approach include the lack of consideration of environmental factors and focusing on processing skills that are not directly related to specific intervention (Torgesen 2002).

This approach to conceptualizing LD differentiates students with an overall profile of low cognitive abilities, as well as low achievement levels (deemed "slow learners" or those with intellectual disability) from those with average IQ levels who struggle to learn specific academic skills. Individuals with below average intelligence levels who do not evidence a discrepancy between abilities, therefore, do not meet criteria for LD based on this approach and require separate methods of intervention. This type of evaluation may elicit specific strengths and weaknesses to aid in individualized intervention strategies or recommendations when the criteria for LD are not met. Using an intra-individual method allows for better identification of higher functioning clients with relative weaknesses than simply looking at levels of performance against established standards. However, this method fails to identify individuals with lower intellectual potential who have significant difficulties but do not show adequate discrepancies between achievement and potential.

The transition to defining specific learning disorder (SLD) in the DSM-5 called for the elimination of the discrepancy model that defined LD for many years, instead focusing on RTI models to determine persistent deficits in a specific area of learning. This model diminishes the need for comprehensive assessment and emphasizes on functional impairment and specific areas of academic difficulty, rather than cognitive deficits associated with poor achievement, integrating the problem-solving and intra-individual approaches. Conceptualization of SLD in this model requires information from multiple sources including the individual's medical, family and developmental history, school history and records, teacher report, parent report, and standardized psychoeducational assessment results.

Important Considerations

When conceptualizing a case with a referral question of learning difficulties, the individual's developmental, medical, and family history should be evaluated to assess for any risk factors associated with neurodevelopmental abnormalities. Evaluators must be cognizant of factors such as complications during labor and delivery, developmental delays, medical conditions, living environment, and family history of LDs or delays. Comprehensive knowledge of an individual's family history can add evidence to the presence of a particular disorder, trait, or behavior. Studies have demonstrated a substantial genetic influence on individual differences in learning abilities such as reading and math, as well as other cognitive abilities like spatial ability and memory (Kovas and Plomin 2007).

Additionally, an individual's psychological functioning can play a large role in the conceptualization and differential diagnosis of LD. Factors that might impact a child's well-being should be examined thoroughly. Symptoms related to various psychological disorders such as mood, anxiety, bipolar, and psychotic disorders often lead to impairment in one's ability to maintain focus, concentration and motivation in class, ultimately leading to poor performance in school. When necessary, structured diagnostic parent and child interviews as well as appropriate clinical rating scales can aid in determining the presence of a clinical disorder. It should be noted that the presence of an LD in childhood increases the risk for comorbid anxiety, depression, poor self-esteem, and suicide in adolescence (Huntington and Bender 1993). Therefore, clinicians should be cautious of attributing poor performance in school solely to one cause and be aware of the increased risk of comorbidity in these conditions.

A comprehensive understanding of biological, psychological, and social contextual factors can provide evidence toward a conceptualization of the etiology of the reported difficulties. Although cognitive processing deficits are found across several disorders, research is limited in the utility of assessment of different cognitive domains in assessment of SLD due to the heterogeneous nature of findings. Therefore, the DSM-5 states that assessment of cognitive processing deficits is not required for this type of evaluation. However, while it is not required, information gathered from comprehensive cognitive evaluation can provide insight into comorbid conditions, such as ADHD, and outline a child's strengths and weaknesses, which may be capitalized upon when creating interventions and providing accommodations.

SLD Criteria from DSM-5

The first symptom required for the diagnosis of SLD is the presence of difficulty learning and using specific academic skills (see Chapter 1 for list of specific skills) that has lasted for at least 6 months, despite the provision of interventions targeting the difficulties. This criterion requires documentation of difficulties learning key academic skills within a formal schooling setting. To fully assess these criteria, teachers should be consulted and described the clear difficulty learning a specific skill. For the difficulties to be considered *persistent*, the individual must show little progress in learning for at least 6 months, even when provided individualized instruction to remediate specific skills. Evidence of persistent learning difficulties can be derived from school records and teacher reports, evaluation of a child's work samples, curriculum-based measures, and clinical interview. It is important to investigate all areas and skills that a child struggles with in order to ensure diagnostic accuracy, including the quality of instruction provided to the child.

The next required diagnostic criterion is that the individual's performance in the targeted area is well below the average level given his or her age. This criterion requires psychometric evidence from tests of academic achievement that are norm- or criterion-referenced. The most basic definition of a deficit in performance is 1.5 standard deviations (SD) below the population mean for the individual's age; however, a more lenient threshold (1.0–2.5 SD) may be applied when learning difficulties are supported by converging evidence from multiple sources. Though comprehensive neuropsychological assessments are not required for diagnosis, the evaluating clinician can gain a wider picture of the individual's functioning across domains to further strengthen conclusions about the nature of specific academic and functional deficiencies. (See Chapter 3 for tests commonly used in SLD evaluations.) For individuals aged 17 years and above, a documented history of impaired learning may be substituted for the standardized assessment; however, clinicians should be wary of gaining information from limited sources and obtain evidence from other sources when possible.

The third feature outlined for SLD is that the specific difficulties in learning can be readily evident in early school years, but may not fully manifest until later school years when learning demands increase and exceed an individual's capacity. The child may perform in the average range on simple tasks in early school years, but struggle in later years with demands such as integrating complex information, completing tests under time limits, completing reading or written assignments with strict deadlines or taking multiple demanding courses. This type of pattern can be assessed through careful consideration of school records and clinical interview. Individuals with above average intellectual functioning may maintain average academic performance through compensatory strategies, such as repetition and memorization, until the learning demand exceeds their abilities or tests become too demanding.

The final feature to be considered when conceptualizing SLD is that the learning difficulties are not better accounted for by other factors that may impede learning due to biological, psychological, or social factors. These should be assessed by the clinician through direct observation, clinical interview, review of medical records, and assessment results combined with clinical judgment. Clinicians should also be aware of common responses to learning struggles, such as frustration, anxiety, and poor self-esteem, which may reinforce task avoidance, leading to further delays in learning. If the disorder is better accounted for by another diagnosis (e.g., anxiety, acquired brain injury), the individual may still qualify for accommodations and services under the alternate diagnosis. If those interventions are focused on the actual underlying problem (rather than the more apparent achievement deficit), there is likely a better long-term outcome for the individual rather than just patching academic difficulties.

Through careful consideration of the criteria for SLD outlined in the DSM-5, the importance of comprehensive evaluation with data from multiple sources is illuminated. The skilled clinician should be able to integrate several sources of data to form hypotheses about an individual's level of academic performance and select appropriate psychometric assessments to support these hypotheses. Accurate diagnoses of an individual's specific LD, along with careful considerations of etiological factors, environmental factors, and the individual's cognitive strengths and weaknesses, can provide the clinician with the tools required for making appropriate, specific, and effective recommendations.

Which Methodology for Assessing SLD Is Better?

When looking at these alternate methods, there are some noted clear strengths and weaknesses. When working with a given entity, we may be required by law or institutional demands to use a certain approach; in such cases, it is incumbent on the clinician to know the criteria and goals of the institutions involved. For example, in South Florida, the school systems require the use of the level of achievement method in order to identify and meet their goal of elevating children whose performances do not meet minimum standards. Some private schools require the use of the discrepancy model (although they differ by whether they accept 1, 1.5, or 2 SD as an adequate discrepancy). Many state professional boards require a clear discrepancy model at 1.5 SD, while others are more flexible with the goal of maximizing the performance of the test taker. The local state college allows both approaches if they can lead to accommodations that will help the student maximize performance, while the state universities are focused on the discrepancy model.

In many cases, the choice of model by institutions is based on their goals. If an institution sees what they are doing as competitive (some people must succeed, while others fail in order to select the best individual), there is likely to be more reliance on the discrepancy model because of a concern of a "level playing field." In such cases, the fear is that giving one student accommodations without rigid standards will allow that individual to get a higher score than deserved, thus giving that individual advantage for being selected in situations where there are real limits to how many people can be accepted or how many can succeed. This is common in competitive school and vocational programs, and especially in high stake tests such as the Scholastic Aptitude Test, Graduate Record Examination, or the Law School Admission Test, among many others.

Other programs have the goal of maximizing performance rather than eliminating or selecting people. Thus, a junior college open to all people may see its mission as attempting to provide an education to everyone and maximizing their success. In such a case, a discrepancy model may not be appropriate. If a student performs poorly, whether due to an SLD, other disorders, low intelligence, or any other factors, the focus should ideally be on maximizing performance rather than a level playing field. In this approach, everyone can succeed equally if they reach the criteria for success. This is especially important in situations where providing accommodations is relatively cost-free, as is the case with many of the accommodations for achievement deficits. In such cases, insisting on rigid definitions and cutoffs makes little sense.

In vocational settings, the law requires reasonable accommodations for individuals with defined deficits. Many businesses insist on a discrepancy model, partly because of fear of the cost of accommodations, disruptions caused by accommodations, or a fear more people will request accommodations. While there are jobs where SLD accommodations would be very difficult and potentially disruptive, other jobs require only minor interventions to help an employee master a job at an acceptable level. In such cases, a broader approach to defining disability would be in the interest of both the employer and the employee. When evaluating a client in these situations, it is important to take an open look at options and when necessary make reasonable accommodation suggestions that benefit everyone involved regardless of the SLD definition being used.

CHAPTER 3

Evaluation and Assessment

Verbal Tests

Verbal abilities require an intricate interplay between a variety of cognitive skills, including receptive and expressive speech, fine motor coordination, reading fluency and comprehension, phonological processing, organization, planning, and word knowledge among other domains. There exists a wide variety of assessments at the clinician's disposal in order to examine these verbal skills. When evaluating a client for a specific learning disability that has been hypothesized to be of a verbal nature, it will be important to consider what to include in the battery of tests to aid in making a proper diagnosis. This is accomplished via having an understanding of the specific referral question, which will influence the particular measures that will be used. In terms of battery selection, it is best to use a flexible battery approach with a few core tests such as the Wechsler Intelligence Scales, Woodcock Johnson Test of Cognitive Abilities (WJ Cog-4th edition; Schrank et al. 2014), and Woodcock Johnson Tests of Achievement (WJ Ach-4th edition; Schrank et al. 2014) along with additional tests that are appropriate for the referral question. Use of a flexible battery approach with general measures and select tests is important so as to provide a thorough analysis of intra- and inter-assessment scores (Bauer 2011). Even still, some clinicians believe longer, more comprehensive tests to be too belaboring for not only the evaluator but also the client. As a result, some clinicians continue to prefer brief measures of reading, spelling, vocabulary, mathematical ability, and other verbal tasks. The following is a summary of popular measures that are frequently used along with other neuropsychological tests. The summaries below are in no way an exhaustive list of measures; however, they can be integral in aiding the examiner in making a diagnosis of a learning disorder (LD).

Wide Range Achievement Test, Fourth Edition

The Wide Range Achievement Test, Fourth Edition (WRAT-4; Wilkinson and Robertson 2006) is one such test that is relatively a brief assessment that measures skills such as word reading ability, spelling, reading comprehension, and arithmetic. This norm-referenced test is available in alternate forms, which allows for serial testing without the concern of practice effects, and has norms available for clients aged 5 to 94 years. Each of the alternate forms (i.e., Green Form and Blue Form) focuses on similar areas of achievement as mentioned above. The WRAT-4 is a relatively versatile assessment tool that can be utilized to assess premorbid intelligence, general reading level and comprehension, writing ability, and mathematical skills. In comparison to larger batteries such as the Wechsler Intelligence and Woodcock-Johnson Scales, the administration time for the WRAT-4 ranges from 15 to 45 minutes, and can be given in a group or individual format.

Like many other neuropsychological measures, the WRAT-4 has specific basal (i.e., minimum number correct) and ceiling rules (maximum number incorrect) that need to be met for each subtest. These cutoffs are colloquially termed the "5/7/10" rules and vary depending on the particular subtest being administered. The rules for word reading are especially important as they determine the starting point for the sentence completion subtest. The minimum number of consecutively correct responses needed in order to waive earlier items on the word reading, spelling, and arithmetic subtests is five items. The discontinuation rule for word reading and spelling subtests is 10 consecutively incorrect items, whereas arithmetic is given 15 minutes to complete as many problems as possible without the use of a calculator. Starting points for sentence completion are determined by the total raw score for word reading, and while the basal rule is the same for sentence completion (i.e., five consecutive items correct), the discontinue rule for this subtest is seven consecutive items incorrect. If the client fails to get *any* of the first five items administered correct, the clinician should test backwards, that is earlier items, from the starting point until the basal is met.

The WRAT-4 is an excellent, brief measure that is useful in estimating premorbid intellectual functioning, writing ability, basic math skills, and comprehension. It may prove useful as a screening measure to help guide additional, more specific tests of achievement. While the WRAT-4 is helpful, it does not evaluate the client on knowledge of words and comprehension of complex and lengthy narratives, which could prompt the clinician to use other measures that assess such abilities.

Nelson Denny Reading Test

Another excellent screening measure for reading ability, reading fluency, and comprehension that clinicians can add to their repertoire of tests is the Nelson Denny Reading Test (NDRT; Nelson, Brown, and Denny 1960). The NDRT is helpful in identifying clients with significant reading issues as well as those that have superior comprehension and vocabulary skills. The NDRT is unique in that it compares the clients' scores to others of a similar grade as opposed to age. This helps the clinician to determine how the individual compares to others with a similar education level. In addition to the use of the NDRT in clinical settings, it has been normed to evaluate police academy recruits, and is often used to predict whether potential candidates will perform well in academic courses at the academy (Brown, Fishco, and Hanna 1993). Like the WRAT-4, the NDRT has two forms (i.e., Forms G and H) that can be used for serial testing to account for practice effects. In contrast to the WRAT-4, this measure contains only two subtests: vocabulary and comprehension (including reading rate). Furthermore, no basal or ceiling cutoffs are used, as scores are contingent on time constraints. The NDRT differs from other reading measures, as it differentiates between standard time and extended time for vocabulary and comprehension.

The vocabulary subtest consists of 80 items of varying levels of difficulty. The client is asked to determine whether a given word is similar to that of one of the multiple-choice items. Standard time for this subtest is 15 minutes and following this time period, the clinician automatically initiates extended time so that she or he will end the subtest after 24 minutes has elapsed in total. In contrast, comprehension consists of 38 items with standard time being 20 minutes and extended time being prolonged to 32 minutes. Furthermore, comprehension involves assessing the client's reading rate, which is determined during the first minute of the comprehension subtest. The client is asked to read at a normal rate, not slower nor faster, and after 1 minute, he or she is asked to indicate the number of the line currently on.

Scoring for vocabulary standard time is the raw score achieved during the designated time, whereas the extended time is the *total* raw score. Similarly, the number of items correctly determines the comprehension subtest raw score during the standard and extended time; however, the raw scores are doubled to determine the *total* raw score. In addition, standard scores and percentiles are determined via the client's level of education attained. It is important for the clinician to indicate what level the client has *completed*. Moreover, the normative data is split between the beginning and end of the year, which, again, is contingent on where the client is in regards to their level of education.

One problem with the NDRT is that scoring is based on educational level rather than age. As a result, there are problems when the results are compared to tests like most intelligence tests whose norms are based on age. If the individual has a 12th grade education level, this does not produce a problem. However, adult individuals with a lower education will get a higher score than expected, because they are being compared to lower IQ people rather than the general population. Similarly, if they have a college or graduate education, their score will be lower than expected because they are compared to a higher IQ population rather than the general population. If the regular norms are used, higher education individuals with above average intelligence will frequently show a discrepancy between IQ and achievement that is not real. A work around suggests the need to compare everyone to the first semester, 13th grade norms that are closest to the general population when comparing to most IQ scores.

In summary, the NDRT is a valuable tool that can be helpful in making a diagnosis of reading disorder. It provides an accurate assessment of the individual's lexical understanding, overall reading rate, and sentence comprehension. In addition, the NDRT allows the clinician to compare the client's performance to others of similar academic level. Furthermore, it allows for an accurate assessment of the client's abilities under time constraints, which can be helpful when making recommendations. This being said, it is important for clinicians to be weary of minimal effort on such tests. Speed and accuracy should be emphasized as clients with prior Individual Education Plan (IEP) may be acclimated to extra time and it is imperative that they work at their quickest speed. In order to have a valid assessment of their reading abilities, clients must perform with optimal effort to determine whether a deficit truly exists.

Gray Oral Reading Test, Fifth Edition

Many clinicians can utilize silent and oral reading assessments to evaluate overall reading skills; however, there are several advantages to using an oral measure as opposed to a silent instrument. For example, oral reading assessments allow examiners to identify how the examinee deciphers letter-sound combinations, process multisyllabic words, and identify phonetically similar or irregular words (Wiederholt and Brown 2012). It is for these reasons that the Gray Oral Reading Test, Fifth Edition (GORT-5) has become a go-to assessment for clinicians that frequently evaluate students with reading impairments. The GORT-5 is a norm-referenced test for adolescents between the ages of 6.0 and 23.11, which evaluates a variety of different reading abilities including reading rate, accuracy of pronunciation of words, fluency, and comprehension. A feature of the GORT-5 that makes it unique among reading instruments is the option to assess for when students substitute a word for the text word. This is a common reading error that is often qualitatively evaluated as opposed to comparing scores to a normative sample.

The GORT-5 is a relatively quick assessment of reading skills that takes approximately 15 to 45 minutes to complete. The GORT-5 begins with the examiner having the student read a story that corresponds to his or her current grade level. This allows the clinician to evaluate the time in which it took the student to complete the story as well as any reading errors that occurred. Following this, the student is asked about the basic comprehension questions regarding the events of the story. The examinee's reading rate and level of accuracy of reading is computed to yield a fluency score. While the GORT-5 assesses multiple aspects of reading, basal and ceiling scores are computed only for fluency. The basal score is established when the student scores 9 to 10 points on two consecutive stories, whereas the ceiling is obtained when the fluency score is 2 or less on two consecutive stories. Reading errors are noted through use of a slash mark system (i.e., when the student mispronounces or misreads a word within the story or when the examinee adds extraneous words). The numbers of slashes are summed to provide the clinician with a total number of deviations from print. The time in which it takes the examinee to read the story provides a rate score, whereas the fluency score is obtained when the rate and accuracy scores are summed.

The GORT-5 is a quick reading assessment that provides clinicians with multiple data points that can be helpful when answering referral questions involving reading ability. Further, it has shown to have excellent reliability and internal validity. In addition, it has been shown to have excellent criterion validity with other popular reading assessments including the NDRT (Brown et al. 1993), Reading Observation Scale (Wiederholt, Hammill, and Brown 2009), Test of Silent Contextual Reading Fluency (Hammill, Wiederholt, and Allen 2006), Test of Silent Reading Efficiency and Comprehension (Wagner et al. 2010), and Test of Silent Word Reading Fluency (Mather et al. 2004). This instrument should be readily available in clinicians' arsenal in order to better understand the level of impairment in reading disorder cases.

Woodcock-Johnson Tests of Achievement, Fourth Edition

One of the most widely used measures when evaluating LDs is the Woodcock-Johnson Tests of Achievement (WJ-Ach 4). This instrument is frequently used in conjunction with the Woodcock-Johnson Tests of Cognitive Abilities (WJ-Cog) and Woodcock-Johnson Tests of Oral Language (WJ-OL), which can help to identify strengths and weaknesses in terms of language abilities along with intellectual skills. This battery of tests consists of a standard set of subtests as well as extended tests for a more comprehensive evaluation of a particular area of interest. A primary reason for the WJ-Ach 4's popularity is its use of Cattell-Horn-Carroll (CHC) theory, which conceptualizes cognitive capacity based on Cattell's original work on crystallized and fluid intelligence (for a better understanding of CHC theory, the astute reader is referred to Schneider and

McGrew [2012] and Flanagan and McGrew [1997]). Further, the authors of the WJ-Ach 4 retained similar reliability and validity coefficients as previous editions of the instrument.

A unique aspect of the WJ-Ach 4 is the normalization of English and Spanish language assessments. This instrument incorporates three broad based clusters of subtests that assess language abilities, which include oral language, broad oral language, and listening comprehension in English and Spanish that make up a comparative language index.

An excellent component of the WJ-Ach 4 is the incorporation of subtests that tap into broad achievement areas that can help with conceptualization of different types of LDs including disorder of written expression and mathematics disorder. As stated above, these subtests can be administered as part of a comprehensive fixed battery or used as part of a flexible battery that is tailored to the individual referral question. These measures can provide the clinician with an understanding of fluency and depth of knowledge surrounding the particular area of interest.

Scoring for all forms of the Woodcock-Johnson requires the clinician to tally a total score for the individual subtest and enter the scores in a computerized scoring system. This helps the scoring process by making it more clinician friendly as well as helps to reduce clinician error when calculating cluster scores. When administering the WJ-Ach 4, evaluators should be conscientious of the different basal and ceiling cutoffs for each of the subtests as they have changed from the WJ-Ach 3, and vary based on the particular test being administered; however, reversal and "test by page" (i.e., continuing to administer items on a page despite the ceiling being met) rules still apply. While new tests have been added to the newest version of the WJ-Ach, similar interpretive guidelines exist, and the astute clinician should consult the test manual for test-specific interpretations as certain subtests (i.e., writing samples) require a certain level of clinical judgment.

Key Math-3 Diagnostic Assessment

When used in conjunction with the WJ-Ach 4, the Key Math-3 Diagnostic Assessment (KM-3 DA) is a helpful tool when there is a concern of a possible mathematics disorder. The core constructs assessed by the KM-3 DA revolve around three components including knowledge and understanding of basic and complex mathematical principles, ability to perform computational tasks, and applying such knowledge to solve advanced mathematical problems (Connolly 2007). The KM-3 DA has shown to be highly reliable and has strong internal consistency, which makes this measurement an excellent instrument to aid clinicians in making the appropriate diagnosis of a mathematics disorder.

The KM-3 DA consists of 10 subtests that assess a wide variety of basic and complex math skills. These subtests include numeration, algebra, geometry, measurement, data analysis and probability, mental computation and estimation, addition and subtraction, multiplication and division, foundations of problem solving, and applied problem solving. There are several aspects of the KM-3 DA that make it a unique tool. First, the examinee's score on the first subtest, numeration, is used as starting points for the remainder of the test. Numeration is an excellent measure to use as a baseline for math skills, which is why it is used to determine start points. This subtest assesses the examinees' ability to identify, compare, and round whole and irrational numbers including fractions, decimal values, and percentages (Connolly 2007). This area of math ability is a foundational skill and without conceptual knowledge of whole and rational numbers, the individual will struggle in many other areas of arithmetic. Another unique aspect of the KM-3 DA includes requiring the examinee to perform mental calculations and judgments regarding problems for all but one subtest. During the applied problem solving subtest, examinees are allowed to use a calculator to aid in solving complex math problems.

The KM-3 DA utilizes age- and grade-based normative data to help clinicians understand where the examinees' abilities fall in comparison to their peers. Norms range from kindergarten to 12th grade, whereas age-based norms range from 4 years 6 months to 21 years 11 months; therefore, it may not be appropriate for examinees who are older. Subtest scores are summed to yield composite index scores, which include basic concepts, operations and applications. Further, a total score is calculated in order to assess the examinee's total math ability.

Conclusion

In summary, the assessments just discussed are popular instruments used by a variety of school psychologists and neuropsychologists to help understand concerns relating to a specific learning disorder (SLD). There are a wide variety of measurements that can be used in making a proper diagnosis of a learning disability; however, discussion of such instruments is beyond the scope of the current chapter. Once a clinician learns the more popular instruments, such as the ones highlighted here, it will be much easier to learn similar tests that assess similar constructs. While tests help to make a diagnosis, it is always important for the astute clinician to gather an in-depth history of academic performance and emotional functioning in order to verify that such a learning disability exists.

Nonverbal Measures

In the evaluation process of a client for LD, it is important to understand the specific referral question, and prior challenges that the client may have. Specifically, issues with verbal abilities may confound results when testing for learning disability if the assessment utilized does not factor this in. The use of nonverbal criteria ensures that the scores for children with specific language impairments are similar to typically developing peer groups (Miller and Gilbert 2008). Assessments such as the Universal Nonverbal Intelligence Test (UNIT) do take this into account and provide the examiner with more specificity to answer the question on the client's intellectual ability and potential learning disability. There are a variety of assessments like the UNIT that are able to assess for LDs and intellectual ability by having little to no verbal direction given by the examiner. Instead, minimal words or hand motions are utilized and taught to the client to better defend against the client's difficulty with verbal abilities confounding the results.

Nonverbal assessments can be beneficial in assessing learning disabilities that may not require verbal abilities, such as understanding of spatial patterns, visual memory, reasoning, ability to plan, graphomotor ability, and so on. A nonverbal assessment can be a good assessment for individuals with SLD, hearing impairment, language impairment, speech impairment, and those whose first language is not English (Roid et al. 2013). A flexible battery can be utilized to assess for learning disabilities through nonverbal assessment. Core subtests can be utilized from the Wechsler Intelligence Scales, the Developmental Neuro Psychological Assessment (NEPSY-II), along with additional assessments that would be appropriate for the referral question. Understanding the referral question and the client is the key here, as these core subtests may be used but there are also full assessments of general ability provided through a nonverbal or minimally verbal approach. The importance is placed on identifying any language impairments, as even nonverbal assessments can still potentially yield poorer results for those with specific language impairment (Swisher, Plante, and Lowell 1994). The following is a summary of popular measures that can be used along with other neuropsychological assessments. The summaries of each assessment below do not indicate a full list of possible nonverbal assessments of learning disability or intellectual ability, but they do provide specific details of measures that can be beneficial in accounting for the client's abilities and making a diagnosis of a LD.

Universal Nonverbal Intelligence Test

The Universal Nonverbal Intelligence Test (UNIT; Bracken and McCallum 1998) offers a full and comprehensive assessment that measures nonverbal intelligence. The UNIT was made for children and adolescents (ages 5 to 17 years) who may have difficulty on verbal measures. The administration of the UNIT provides a nonverbal approach to testing for general intelligence and cognitive abilities. This offers a fair assessment of intelligence for those who have difficulties with language and speech as well as hearing impairments. The UNIT is a good measure of intelligence for those who cannot communicate verbally, those who have difficulty with language due to different cultural backgrounds, and for individuals who have deficiency in visual perception. The UNIT has also been made to be able to examine educational disabilities, such as LDs and psychiatric disorders.

The UNIT is organized through six subtests that measure memory and reasoning. There are three subtests in each category of memory and reasoning. Memory subtests include symbolic memory, object memory, and spatial memory. Symbolic memory is a 30-item test that provides the examinee with a sequence of symbols said to be universal. The examinee is exposed to the symbols and is to recreate the sequence seen. The test is discontinued after five consecutive scores of zero, or a score of zero on both items one and two. This subtest is utilized to measure short-term visual memory and complex sequential memory. Object memory measures short-term recognition and recall through the identification of up to 30 scored items. The examinee chooses appropriate pictures from an initial array of images, which are then changed in a second viewing to include more objects. Spatial memory is a measure of short-term visual memory. In this subtest, the examinee is asked to recreate up to 27 scored spatial patterns of green, black, or green and black dots that are exposed for 5 seconds. Spatial memory follows the same discontinue rule as symbolic memory and object memory.

The reasoning subtests include analogic reasoning, cube design, and mazes. Analogic reasoning measures symbolic reasoning by having the examinee complete up to 31 scored items of conceptual or geometric analogies. The analogies are within a matrix and one of four possible responses must be chosen. Analogic reasoning is stopped after five consecutive scores of zero. Cube design is a time-limited measure visual spatial reasoning. It measures the ability to reconstruct a potential 15-item scored design made with green-and-white cubes from an original stimulus. Cube design is discontinued after three consecutive scores of zero, or if a basal score of zero is established on both item one and two. Mazes are a measure of reasoning and measuring the ability to plan. This is measured by having the examinee trace a path through a maze to an exit point. The mazes become more complex as the administration continues. Mazes include up to 13 scored items and are discontinued after a raw score of zero or one on three consecutive scored mazes. Each maze is time limited and when the time limit is hit, the examiner stops the examinee from proceeding with the maze.

The six subtests scores are utilized to create five standardized scales with a mean of 100 and a standard deviation of 15. The five scales are Memory Quotient (MQ), Reasoning Quotient (RQ), Symbolic Quotient (SQ), Nonsymbolic Quotient (NSQ), and Full Scale Intelligence Quotient (FSIQ). The FSIQ is analogous to that of the Wechsler Intelligence

Scales, as it provides an overall cognitive and intellectual functioning measure. MQ is an index for short-term recall and recognition. MQ measures content, location, and sequence. RQ is a measure of abilities to plan, understand relationships, and process patterns thoughtfully. The SQ index measures ability to solve problem through organization, categorization, and internal voice to mediate how to proceed with a task. The NSQ index measures the solution of abstract material within problems that are not considered to be meaningful or easily solved through verbal mediation.

The UNIT is an excellent measure that is useful in establishing current intellectual functioning through memory and ability to reason through tasks. The UNIT is administered without verbal direction. It is instead administered through the use of gestures such as head nodding, head shaking, palm rolling, open-handed shrugging, pointing, hand waving, stop, and thumbs up. With the UNIT being completely nonverbal specifically for assessment, it is appropriate with both language-based and nonverbal-learning disabilities. Since it does not require spoken language, the UNIT is appropriate for an assessment of intellectual functioning for children and adolescents with communicative disorders such as expressive language disorder. While the UNIT is helpful, the universal gestures and body language may be unknown by the examinee. As well, there is no specific script for administration, which allows room for nonstandardized administrations.

Test of Nonverbal Intelligence, Fourth Edition

The Test of Nonverbal Intelligence, Fourth Edition (TONI-4; Brown, Sherbenov, and Johnsen 2010) is an individual assessment of general intelligence. The TONI-4 is a brief measure as it takes approximately 15 minutes to administer. It is able to assess intelligence in children and adolescents who have difficulty with language or motor skills. These deficits may confound results in other assessments of cognitive ability that are more verbal in nature. The TONI-4 has both verbal and nonverbal instructions as well as instructions in several foreign languages. The TONI-4 utilizes figural problem solving subtests and subtests for abstract reasoning to estimate general intelligence.

The TONI-4, an assessment of general intelligence for those who have hearing, language, or motor impairment, was designed to be used with children and adults. The ages range from 6 to 89 years of age. This assessment is utilized not only for estimating general intelligence, but also for identifying intellectual impairment, ruling out intellectual concerns in those who have language or motor impairments, and for formulating future interventions. The format of the TONI-4 consists of an untimed approach where the examiner must choose between oral or nonverbal directions. Nonverbal instructions are uniform to maintain a proficient estimate of cognitive ability without the possibility of confounding results. The nonverbal instructions advise the examiner to point at an empty box within the utilized picture book. The examiner then shifts the examinees focus to the first response choice and shake their head "no" or "yes" across the different possible choices to have the examinee understand how to make an appropriate response. When there appears to be a clear under-standing of the process by examinees, they are asked to complete training items and then the full task.

The TONI-4 utilizes a picture book that consists of two different forms, A or B. After the test is taught in a similar fashion to what is seen in matrix reasoning within the Wechsler Intelligence Scale for Children (WISC) or Wechsler Adult Intelligence Scale (WAIS), the examinee is to proceed through each set of six possible answers to insert into the miss-ing piece of the puzzle. If performed nonverbally, the examiner points to the missing piece and then scans his or her finger across the possible choices and then back to the blank box. The examinee then points out their answers. The basal for the TONI-4 is five consecutive correct items starting at item 1 for ages 6 to 9 years and item 20 for ages 10 years or older. The ceiling for the TONI-4 is three incorrect responses within five consecutive items administered. The examinee also gets six training items administered to make sure that they understanding the process and rules of the assessment. Each item beyond the training items is scored as a "one" for correct or "zero" for incorrect. This allows for the obtainment of a raw score.

The raw score on the TONI-4 is then converted to an index score. Index scores then give percentile rank that accounts for the percentage of the normative sample that scored equal to or below the examinee's score.

The index score is divided into categories from "Very Superior" to "Very Poor." The index score matches the same distribution of scores seen on other assessments of intelligence such as the WISC and Stanford-Binet Intelligence Scales. Therefore, for the TONI-4, a score of 90 to 110 is considered average, with a mean of 100 and a standard deviation of 15. The TONI-4 also obtains an age equivalent for the examinee's score to show the examinee's mental age.

The TONI-4 is another useful test to account for intelligence and potential learning disabilities through the utilization of a nonverbal approach. The TONI-4 in itself cannot diagnose but is another component that can be utilized to obtain a fair score of intelligence. It can determine if there are prior language deficits, developmental aphasia, hearing impairment or deafness, and speech or motor deficits. The TONI-4 also does not utilize cultural symbols or pictures that may benefit in the testing of those with different language and cultural backgrounds. The current normative sample for the TONI-4, however, is based on English speakers with 77 percent, given the assessment utilizing the English oral instructions, and only 23 percent were using the nonverbal instructions. This should be taken into account with future iterations and research on the TONI. The TONI-4 is though said to be valid and reliable for assessment of children, adolescents, and adults.

Leiter International Performance Scale, Third Edition

The Leiter International Performance Scale, Third Edition (Leiter-3; Roid et al. 2013) is an individual assessment of cognitive functioning in individuals from the ages of 3 to 75+ years old. It has measures of nonverbal intelligence through the assessment of fluid reasoning and visualization. The Leiter-3 also measures nonverbal intelligence through assessment of nonverbal memory, attention, and cognitive interference. It was developed as a measure of cognitive functioning for groups of individuals consisting of significant communication disorders, autism, cognitive delay, learning disabilities, motor impairment, traumatic brain injury, hearing impairments, and for those whose first language is not English.

Similar to the other discussed nonverbal assessments, the Leiter-3 also consists of nonverbal instructions where the examiner pantomimes to the examinee. This consists of head and hand movements, and facial expressions within the demonstration so that the examinee understands the nature of the subtest. The examiner initially gets the examinees attention through the use of focused eye contact and hand signals. The examiner then can demonstrate pointing to the stimulus book by pointing back and forth between the card and stimulus picture within the subtest to be able to teach appropriately pointing to the correct answer. The examiner can also utilize facial expression of questioning to elicit a response from the examinee. This would occur after a cue for response and can be done by establishing eye contact with the examinee. The examiner then gestures toward the card with an open hand and raising an eyebrow to elicit a similar response such as asking the question, "What is the answer?" The examiner also continues to point back and forth between the response book and stimulus to draw the examinees attention and show how to progress through the subtest with the help of training questions.

The Leiter-3 consists of 10 subtests that are distributed into two groups. All subtests have a restart rule where if the examinee cannot get the correct answer at start, even after teaching, the examiner will then proceed with the preceding age group starting point. The Cognitive Battery groups consist of five subtests measuring nonverbal intellectual ability that is related to reasoning. Of the five subtests, only four need to be administered and it will take an examiner approximately 45 minutes for this administration. The five subtests included in the Cognitive Battery are classification or analogies, sequential order, figure ground, form completion, and visual patterns. Figure ground engages the examinee in identifying figures within a complex stimulus. The subtest ends with there are six failed responses overall. Form completion measures the ability to recognize a whole object from parts that are displayed to the examinee in a random fashion. Form completion ends when there are seven collective failed responses. Classification or analogies test the examinee through the use of matrix analogies that utilize geometric shape. This subtest has a ceiling of seven collective responses failed. Sequential order is a test of correctly selecting stimuli that should progress within a certain order. Sequential order has a ceiling of seven cumulative responses failed. Visual patterns is an optional subtest to be used if one of the other four core subtests in the Cognitive Battery is said to be compromised and needs to be thrown out. Visual patterns have a unique restart rules with examinees receiving a score of zero if they cannot independently provide a correct answer at the starting point. As well visual patterns have a unique ceiling with five cumulative failed responses for ages 3 to 5 years and six cumulative failed responses for ages 6 to 75 years.

The Leiter-3 has an Attention or Memory Battery that consists of the other five subtests. This includes two memory subtests, two nonverbal attention subtests, and the Stroop subtest. The Attention or Memory Battery can be administered within 30 minutes and provides nonverbal measures of cognitive deficits. The five subtests included in the Attention or Memory Battery are: Attention and Interference, Attention Sustained, Nonverbal Stroop, Forward Memory, and Reverse Memory. There is also an optional subtest called Attention Divided.

Attention Sustained has the examinee find and cross out certain squares contained in an array of geometric shapes that become progressively harder to decipher. The subtest is ended only if the examinee doesn't understand the task during the teaching trials. This subtest also has a time limit with all pages having either a 30- or 60-second time limit denoted. Forward Memory has the examinee provide a specific pattern of recall to remember a sequence of picture presented to him or her. The examinee must then repeat the sequence. The subtest ends when there are six failed sequences overall. Attention Divided is a measure of being able to handle multiple tasks by having the examinee place colored foam circles in a corresponding colored bowl. This is to be done while the examinee should also do another task of slapping only red triangles within an arrangement of sorting cards as they are flipped over by the examiner at a rate of one card per second. The subtest is ended when the task is completed, as appropriate for the age group. Reverse Memory has the examinee remember a sequence of pictures within the opposite order that the examiner pointed to them and is ended when six cumulative sequences are failed. Nonverbal Stroop is a test of cognitive ability conducted not in the usual manner of the Stroop but rather by having the examiner use nonverbal cues to indicate that an individual should cross out as many pictures as possible that look like a target image. Both Color Congruent and Color Incongruent tasks of the Nonverbal Stroop have 45-second time limits that are recorded as the examinee ends the task.

Similar to other nonverbal assessments discussed, the Leiter-3 provides scaled scores with a mean of 10 and a standard deviation of 3 for each sub-test, and a composite score of IQ that has a mean of 100 and a standard deviation of 15. Both batteries should be used together for thoughtful and thorough assessment. This is of importance when the assessment of functioning is related to cognitive deficits in memory or attention that are interfering with scores. IQ scores can come in three forms for the Leiter-3 with the normalized score, a deviation IQ, and as a standard score. Non-verbal IQ comes from the Cognitive Battery, while Nonverbal Memory and Processing Speed come from the Attention or Memory Battery. There are also five special supplemental scores available. These are: Attention Sustained (total correct and total errors), Attention Divided (correct and incorrect), Nonverbal Stroop Congruent (incorrect), and Nonverbal Stroop Incongruent (incorrect). Scores on the Leiter-3 compare well to the Stanford Binet as well to measure cognitive ability.

Research on the Leiter-3 has focused on nonverbal assessment, as individuals with disorders such as autism, deafness, speech impairment, intellectual deficiency, adult dementia, stroke affecting communication abilities, and selective mutism may be able to receive a better estimate of intellectual ability or potential learning disability. For best testing of learning disability through this nonverbal assessment, it is important to understand how the examinee usually communicates, what alternative ways has the examinee been able to communicate, and understanding what adaptations need to be made to the testing environment. Adap-tations such as understanding if separation from a caregiver will cause a problem or how long the examinee can tolerate testing before a break are important to know. As well, the examiner should understand physical strengths and limitations an examinee has, and if he or she has had prior assessment. Prior assessment is important to determine what modifica-tions to testing have proved to be successful for an examinee who, for example, may have a speech deficit.

Peabody Picture Vocabulary Test, Third Edition

The Peabody Picture Vocabulary Test, Fourth Edition (PPVT-4; Dunn and Dunn 2007) is a measure of receptive vocabulary in children, adolescents, and adults. In the PPVT-4, the examinee is shown four colored pictures arranged on a page. The examinee is then asked to select the picture that best fits the meaning of a stimulus word said by the examiner. The PPVT-4 consists of a total of 228 items and training items both in Forms A and B of the assessment. The PPVT-4 is a brief assessment, lasting about 10 to 15 minutes, and it is scored while the assessment is ongoing. The PPVT-4 does not require expressive language but rather is an evaluation of the examinee's comprehension of acquired vocabulary. The PPVT-4 is useful among nonreaders and individuals with written language difficulties as it requires no reading or writing. As well, for examinees with expressive language difficulties, the PPVT-4 solely measures linguistic potential since its format is purely receptive in nature.

The PPVT-4 is an untimed test of vocabulary. Examinees are usually encouraged after 10 seconds to give a response to the examiner's stimulus word. Examinees are only tested on their critical range of items with approximately 5 sets of items or 60 items in total. The examiner is encouraged to record special considerations for testing such as an examinee's language background, information about hearing or visual acuity, or if testing is modified to suit the needs of an examinee. The PPVT-4 is beneficial as a nonverbal assessment in assessing hearing vocabulary, as the examinees are not required to say their answer. Instead, during the PPVT-4 the examinees can show their answer by pointing to what they believe is correct. For examinees who will require or benefit from pointing their responses, the examiner should indicate in the first few stimulus words that the response should be pointed at by saying, "Put your finger on …," or "Point to … ." In more difficult settings, such as an examinee with severe motor or speech impairment, the examiner may point to each response option on the Item Page and ask the examinee to use a head shake or an indicated response, such as a blink for a "yes," to indicate positive or negative response. A communication board may be utilized as well.

The recommended start item for the PPVT-4 is chosen by the examinee's age. The starting point is set, as it indicates the point where about 85 percent of examinees within that age group were able to meet the basal set criterion of 11 or 12 items correct within the first administered set. In the basal set, the examinee is to score either one or zero errors. If this rule is not met, the set should continue to be administered then drop back to the previous set to administer all 12 items within that set. The ceiling set is established as the highest set of items administered containing eight or more errors. The assessment is then discontinued at this time. Raw scores are established by subtracting the number of errors from the ceiling item. The PPVT-4 utilizes a deviation and developmental normative score. The standard score on the PPVT-4 has a mean score of 100 and a standard deviation of 15 for a score for the person's age or grade.

With the special considerations made for individuals with difficulties of expressive language, the PPVT-4 can be a beneficial assessment of acquired vocabulary. As opposed to other assessments where individuals with expressive language difficulties may not perform well, the PPVT-4 offers these special considerations, such as pointing at the correct answer to create a better understanding of the individual's strengths and weaknesses. The PPVT-4 does have some drawbacks, as the test is not good for non-English speakers given that there is still verbalization from the examiner. Therefore, there must be some auditory comprehension of what the examiner is describing. As well, it should be noted that PPVT-4 is only a measure in hearing vocabulary and therefore results should not be overstated.

Wechsler Nonverbal Scale of Ability

The Wechsler Nonverbal Scale of Ability (WNV; Wechsler and Naglieri 2006) was designed for individuals with language disorders, deaf or hard of hearing, and individuals who do not speak English. The WNV tried to provide a fair assessment of knowledge for individuals belonging to one of these groups. The WNV was made as a modification to the original Wechsler Scales as seen in the WISC and WAIS. The WNV expanded these assessments to those with language constraints as it gives these examinees a fair look at their intellectual ability.

The WNV has six subtests: Matrices, Coding, Object Assembly, Recognition, Spatial Span, and Picture Arrangement. Subtests have been placed into two age brackets as not all tests are appropriate for certain ages. The ages for each battery are 4 to 7 years and 8 to 21 years. Both age batteries have a four- and two-subtest model, as well. For ages 4 to

7 years, the two-subtest battery includes Matrices and Recognition. The four-subtest battery includes Matrices, Coding, Object Assembly, and Recognition.

Matrices are a subtest that requires the examinee to distinguish different shapes and geometric designs through spatial or logical organization. From there, the examinee is to select the best piece to complete the relationship among the shapes or design. Matrices are a good measure of ability involving perceptual reasoning and simultaneous processing. Matrices can be done completely by having the examinee point to the correct answer. Coding is a subtest that requires the examinee to now copy symbols that are paired with shapes or numbers. It is a time-limited test of 120 seconds. Coding is a good measure of general ability involving graphomotor speed. The Object Assembly subtest has the examinee assemble a variety of puzzle pieces to form recognizable objects. The amount of pieces varies within the subtest from two to eight. Object Assembly provides a good assessment of organization and reasoning. Recognition is the last subtest in the 4 to 7 years of age battery. Recognition requires the examinee to look at a stimulus for 3 seconds and then choose the response option that was identical to the stimulus image shown. The Recognition subtest provides the examiner with an interpretable subtest of immediate memory.

For the battery given to children aged 8 to 21, the two-subtest battery includes Matrices and Spatial Span. The four-subtest battery includes Matrices, Coding, Spatial Span, and Picture Arrangement. Coding gets a different format with using numbers one to nine instead of shapes to pair with the copied symbols. The two new subtests for this age group are Spatial Span and Picture Arrangement. Spatial Span has the examinee reproduce a sequence of blocks tapped by the examiner. The examinee is, however, to produce the order in the same or reverse order of what was demonstrated by the examiner. Spatial Span is a good measure of working memory with visual-spatial stimuli. Picture Arrangement has the examinee arrange illustrated cards of an event in the correct order to tell a story. Picture Arrangement gives the examiner data on how the examinee does with interpreting information and utilizes organization.

The WNV converts raw scores into standard scores. These standard scores are later translated into Full Scale scores. The Full Scale score has a mean of 100 and a standard deviation of 15, which keeps it attune with other Wechsler assessments of intellectual ability. The WNV also utilizes age- and grade-based normative data to help clinicians understand where the examinees' abilities fall in comparison to their peers. The WNV also does well with populations of the deaf or hard of hearing. With brief phrases for standard directions, the WNV doesn't deviate much from the standard administration when administering the assessment to those who are deaf or hard of hearing. For the WNV, the examiner is also allowed to use American Sign Language and cued speech through eight hand movements, all meaning a certain action.

Conclusion

In summary, the nonverbal assessments discussed are popular instruments that are used by a variety of practitioners including neuropsychologists and school psychologists. These nonverbal assessments help to give the examiner a better understanding for difficulty related to an SLD that may have been misrepresented when given an assessment that is not attune to the examinee's strengths and needs. It is important to note that while these assessments help in the process of diagnosis, it is important for the examiner to be understanding of the examinee's performance in academic settings and at home. As well, understanding the examinee's need for nonverbal assessment should be accounted for through multiple sources beyond testing. The assembly of all of these pieces of information will yield the best results for understanding if the client indeed does have a learning disability.

Assessments for Special Populations

Specialized methods and interpretation of testing must be considered for those with sensory and physical limitations. Sensory disabilities can include limitations in sight or hearing, while physical limitations may range from slight motor incoordination to absence of limbs. In general, standardized test administration is altered when providing testing accommodations for special populations; however, important information can still be gained. Alterations in standardized test administration must be documented carefully, and results should be interpreted with the person's level of impairment considered.

When evaluating an individual with disabilities, the clinician should consider the etiology of the individual's limitations, the extent of his or her disability, and other comorbid conditions that may impact testing results. These considerations should be documented within the context of the findings, and hypotheses should be clearly outlined due to the nonstandardized procedures utilized. According to the Individuals with Disabilities Education Improvement Act (IDEA; Turnbull et al. 2009) and DSM-5, a specific learning disability does not include learning problems that are primarily the result of visual, hearing, or motor disabilities. The assessment results must show a discrepancy beyond the sensory or physical limitation in order to warrant a diagnosis of a learning disability.

Assessments for the Hearing Impaired

Before beginning the assessment, alterations in the testing environment should be made to ensure that visual and auditory disturbances are minimized, as hearing-impaired individuals are more sensitive to these types of distractions (Hällgren et al. 2001). Alterations may include choosing a room without a window, turning down noisy air conditioners or fans, and preventing distracting interruptions.

When conducting assessments with deaf or partially deaf individuals, the presentation of oral information must be altered to match the person's preferred manner of communication. Oral instructions should not be provided to those who primarily communicate through American Sign Language or through other visual communication. Although an individual may informally utilize speech reading, this method has been proven to be inaccurate and requires increased cognitive load, which can lead to inaccurate results (de Filippo 1982).

When presenting hearing-impaired individuals with instructions in their preferred medium, limitations in vocabulary may lead to inaccurate translations and increase the chance of misinterpretation of the instructions. Extra care should be taken to carefully model tasks or provide extra practice trials to ensure that the individual has understood what is required (Hill-Briggs et al. 2007).

While it is ideal that the clinician perform the evaluation in the client's preferred mode of communication, this is not always feasible. In cases when an interpreter is necessary, an interpreter with extensive experience in mental health interpreting is preferred in order to preserve the intended purpose of the tests (Vernon and Miller 2001). The evaluator should consult with the interpreter to further understand the individual's patterns of strengths and weaknesses in his or her preferred language and utilize that information in conceptualization. The interpreter should be aware of subtle language errors, such as phonological errors that might otherwise be overlooked.

Selecting Tests for the Hearing Impaired

The evaluating clinician should be aware of several issues when selecting tests for the hearing-impaired or deaf individual. Depending on the level of impairment, tests requiring significant verbal skills may be inappropriate due to poor access to the required knowledge base. Historically, the Wechsler Performance scales have been utilized to estimate deaf individuals' intelligence level; however, this method is susceptible to over- or underestimate intellectual levels, especially when assessing LDs (Braden 1994). Using this method may cause those with nonverbal LDs to look more impaired, and may overlook those with verbal LDs. Hill-Briggs et al. (2007) provide recommendations for the use of commonly used tests with deaf or hearing-impaired individuals, along with considerations specific to this population.

For intelligence tests (e.g., WISC-V), they suggest limiting evaluations to the performance tests assuming the examiner can properly communicate the instructions. They recommend that only clinicians experienced with deaf populations should attempt to give the verbal scales. Interpretation should be limited to the functional areas that are directly assessed in the nonverbal tests. Fluid reasoning tests using spatial relationships may be appropriate, but again the issue of communicating instructions must be considered.

For the achievement tests, they indicate that tests of auditory comprehension should clearly be omitted. Use of executive function tests will vary; those dependent on language or hearing or words should be avoided in most circumstances, focusing on those tests that are nonverbal in nature. Measures like the Trail Making Test, which assumes automaticity of the alphabet, may produce meaningless results, as would language-based tests like the Stroop Color and Word Test. Instruments like the Wisconsin Card Sorting Test, maze tasks, figural fluency, and other nonverbal tests are more appropriate assuming that instructions can be reliably and accurately communicated.

For Digit Span, deaf users generally show equivalent forward and backward scores, rather than the normal advantage of forward. Visual span norms are appropriate for the hearing impaired. Memory tests that focus on nonverbal material without any verbal response are appropriate. Verbal tests conveyed by signing may be altered based on differences between signing and spoken tests, so probably should be avoided unless one is proficient in working with this population. Recall of stories and sentences will likely be difficult for the client; if used, the scores are best compared to verbal IQ rather than overall functioning. Attentional tests that use nonverbal symbols are generally OK, but those that use letters or verbal materials will yield inconsistent results.

For motor or sensory tests, one should avoid those that require a blindfold—a barrier can be used instead if this is possible, but measures like the Tactual Performance Test should be avoided. Visual-Motor tests such as the Rey Complex Figure and Bender-Gestalt should be interpreted primarily on the basis of whether the items are distorted, not the organizational process used. The Rorschach can be administered in sign language, but there are no separate norms for such administrations. Verbal tests of personality like the Minnesota Multiphasic Personality Inventory will often be distorted because of both the verbal contact and the experiences of the hearing impaired individual.

When administering the tests to the deaf population, several administrative cautions should be followed: (1) Ensure testing environment is free from distracting auditory and visual stimuli. (2) Alter presentation of oral information to match the examinee's preferred manner of communication. (3) Avoid allowing the examinee to utilize lip-reading, as this method is proven to be inaccurate. (4) Carefully model tasks or provide extra practice trials to ensure directions are fully understood. (5) Utilize a trained interpreter when possible to ensure accurate results are obtained, although an examiner fluent in sign language is preferred. (6) Tests with a significant verbal component may be inappropriate for hearing-impaired or deaf individuals. (7) Norms for the general population may not be accurate.

Assessments for the Blind

Assessment of individuals with significant visual impairment or blindness is limited due to the emphasis on visual formats of widely used tests. Additionally, the heterogeneous nature of visual impairment has provided challenges in developing normative data for tests to be used with this population. Efforts to construct a comprehensive assessment battery for individuals with visual impairments led to the development of the Comprehensive Vocational Education System (CVES), which has been used in clinical, vocational, and educational assessments within a visually impaired population and includes a large normative sample ranging from ages 15 to 69 years (Dial et al. 1991). This battery provides measures of verbal-spatial cognitive abilities, perceptual-motor functions, and emotional-coping concerns.

Hill-Briggs et al. (2007) made several recommendations regarding clients with visual difficulties. Verbal tests from instruments like the WISC-V and the WAIS-IV may be administered without any modifications. Clearly, nonverbal tests of any kind requiring visual skills cannot be given. They recommend use of the Cognitive Test for the Blind (CTB), which includes textured and raised materials, a response board, and a screen for clients who may have limited visual skills. The WRAT has versions available in large print for those with partial sight or in Braille with the version sued dependent on the preferential style of the individual. The Hepatic Sensory Discrimination Test offers appropriate norms, textured and rubber stimulus materials, a screen for those with limited visual skills, and alternate (hands-on) methods of demonstration and instruction.

They also recommend the McCarron Assessment of Neuromuscular Development, which has a version for the visually impaired. The CVES provides a battery of tests that have been modified for use in this population, and normative data for ages 15 to 69 years. They also suggest a variety of instruments to measure emotional status and coping. All of these tests have norms for the visually impaired or blind along with oral or large print versions. These tests include the Observational Emotional Inventory, the Emotional Behavioral Checklist, the Minnesota Multiphasic Personality Inventory, the Rotter Incomplete Sentence Blank, the Beck Depression Inventory (BDI), Beck Anxiety Inventory (BAI), and the Survey of Functional Adaptive Behavior. As noted before, the sensory impairment should not be the underlying cause, but occur concomitantly with the SLD.

In children, good visual clarity and resolution are necessary for discerning small print. However, there is no evidence that children with moderate myopia, moderate hyperopia, or moderate astigmatism have any greater difficulty in learning to read than children without eyesight difficulties (Handler and Fierson 2011). Children with unrecognized and untreated hyperopia (farsightedness) may appear uninterested in books, and secondarily delay the onset of reading behaviors; however, this type of delay has not been linked to disorders of reading (Martin 2004). In order to provide accurate assessments, children who evidence mild visual impairment should be referred for a visual examination.

General recommendations of this population include: (1) Normative data is limited for the visually impaired or blind population due to the heterogeneous nature of visual impairment. (2) Common modifications for visually impaired individuals include adding textured stimuli, large print or Braille, verbal rather than written instructions and hands on demonstration. (3) When diagnosing a learning disability, the impairment must be found to extend beyond the visual impairment.

Assessments for Those with Motor Difficulties

Motor difficulties may impact the extent to which one can complete standardized assessments and tests. Several conditions can affect both fine and gross motor functioning. Congenital conditions such as Cerebral Palsy, as well as acquired injuries to the brain or spinal cord can impact physical functioning and alter performance on standardized assessment measures. Peripheral injury or motor incoordination can also impair performance on tests requiring motor output. Impairment in motor functioning can affect abilities necessary for testing, such as gripping or grasping objects, writing, pointing, or drawing. As the focus of an LD assessment is not to determine the extent of the physical impairment, alternate means of responding should be provided during testing when appropriate.

Accommodations for individuals with physical impairment include modifying the test presentation format, response modality, time allotted, and selection of tests (AERA, APA, NCME, Joint Committee on Standards for Educational, and Psychological Testing [U.S.] 1999). Research and normative data for the assessment of physically impaired individuals is sparse due to the widely held view that the testing modifications are less problematic than those for other disabilities (Lezak 2004). Therefore, common practices for providing accommodations for this population are based on clinical judgment and experience (Geisinger et al. 2011).

Hill-Briggs et al. (2007) suggested multiple accommodations for individuals with motor impairment including such issues as pain, fatigue, and accessibility. These recommendations include: (1) adjustment of time limits or elimination of speed tests or both; (2) administration of portion of test that does not require skills affected by disability (e.g., omit tests like Block Design); (3) oral administration and responding rather than self-administration (e.g., BDI, BAI); (4) substitution of tests that do not require motor response; (5) use of adaptive equipment to facilitate motor responding when there is residual motor function (e.g., pencil grips, paper or document holders); (6) use of adaptive equipment to compensate for absent motor response (e.g., head stick, light beam, switching mechanism, and computers); (7) use of an unaffected nondominant hand; (8) allowing breaks, positioning changes to minimize fatigue; (9) schedule during the best times for the clients energy level; (10) shorter sessions; (11) special chairs or other alternate seating as most appropriate for the client; (12) ensuring a work surface that allows ease of reach, resting of an affected hand or arm and arm braces or splints; (13) a table with tilt and fasteners to hold materials to be viewed in place; (14) accessible test location with accessible ancillary facilities (building, restroom, and cafeteria or eating area) and fully accessible room; (15) tables adjusted to accommodate wheelchair size.

Research with spinal cord injury survivors provides examples of test selection and alterations for motor-free assessment (Dowler et al. 1997). Tests frequently used in comprehensive assessments include: the Wechsler

Memory Scale (WMS) omitting the Visual Reproduction subtest, the WAIS and WISC verbal subtests, Symbol Digit Modalities Test, the Rey Auditory Verbal Learning Test, the California Verbal Learning test, the Stroop Test, the Benton Visual Retention Test, Benton Facial Recognition Test, Halsted Category Test, Judgment of Line Orientation, Hooper Visual Organization Test, and Controlled Oral Word Association Test (Hill-Briggs et al. 2007). Additionally, achievement tests may be altered to allow the individual to provide answers orally, rather than writing them.

It is important to note that the etiology of the physical impairment as well as comorbid conditions play a joint role in test performance. For example, cerebral palsy is often comorbid with learning disability (Shapiro 2004). The evaluator should remain careful in their interpretations when accommodating disabilities by omitting tests and domains to avoid overlooking a comorbid condition.

The clinical interpretation of test results should reflect the evaluator's comprehensive analysis of etiology, age at onset, extent of disability or level of functioning, comorbid conditions, and how these factors, independently and in combination, impact performance on assessments. It is important to interpret findings in the context of the test administration procedures or response formats used. Interpretation should also incorporate any physical discomfort or distress reported at the time of testing. All modifications to standardized test procedures should be clearly described in the report of findings.

Overall, motor impairment can range from mild fine motor incoordination to complete loss of limb functioning, so accommodations need to be appropriate to the individual. These may include modifying the test presentation format, allowing alternate response modalities, altering the time allotted, and selecting alternative assessments. Interpretation should be carefully considered so that motor issues are not confused with cognitive difficulties. Comorbid conditions such as depression or anxiety should be considered as possible causes in addition to cognitive problems; despite the slowness of the evaluation in some motor disorders, comprehensive evaluations remain necessary. All modifications to standardized test procedures should be clearly described in the report of findings.

CHAPTER 4

Interventions

Brief Introduction to IEP

Students who meet criteria for a specific learning disability (SLD) or other forms of disability may qualify for an individual education plan (IEP) and become eligible for special education and related services. An IEP attempts to help students achieve educational goals more easily than they are able to on their own (Kupper 2000). Schools must provide a written account for each student with a disability that is developed, reviewed, and revised in accordance with codes 300.320 through 300.324 of Federal Regulations of the Offices of the Department of Education. In all cases, the IEP must be individualized to account for particular needs as identified by the IEP evaluation, and must help teachers and related personnel understand the student's disability and how the disability affects the learning process. IEPs, per se, are not required in vocational or postsecondary settings but the same principles apply with the emphasis on maximizing performance. Primary and secondary schools, however, generally have a legal requirement to go much further than employers or other institutions in terms of how far they are expected to go to help the individual because of a legal commitment to a fair and comprehensive education for everyone regardless of disability. It should also be remembered that the presence of other disabilities (e.g., diabetes and seizure disorder) may require additional accommodations beyond the type described here. These suggestions go beyond the official diagnostic categories to suggest other areas that need to be addressed. There is, as well, some duplication of accommodations across disabilities, and the reader may always borrow ideas from other areas if they aid a specific student.

Academic Accommodations for Students with Specific Learning Disorders

The academic success of students with learning disorders is dependent on appropriate and individualized accommodations made to class instruction as well as other school-based activities. Such accommodations often involve changes to the classroom environment and may provide alternate methods, supports, or task adaptations to course material (Beech 2010). In many instances, students with specific learning disorders need accommodations for particular types of classroom assignments or instructional presentations. Furthermore, some students may require a combination of accommodations to facilitate task completion and promote academic success. In order for such students to achieve optimal growth, it is essential that relevant adaptations, accommodations, and modifications be based upon their personal needs, learning styles, and interests. This chapter is devoted to helping parents, teachers, and others find information that can guide appropriate changes in the classroom based on what their students need.

One of the first steps in developing appropriate academic accommodations is identifying the particular task(s) a student struggles with and is unable to perform autonomously. Members of the IEP team must then ask why such tasks are difficult for the student and determine which accommodation(s) will help their performance (Gerlach, Murphy, and Dasta 2009). This is accomplished by analyzing the key parts of such tasks, which may involve cognitive, motor, sensory, social, emotional, and communication processes to carry them out (Zabala 2010). It is important that the specific components of accommodations match the student's capabilities and needs in these domains. The next step includes identifying the expected grade-level or age-appropriate performance for the key parts of the task. Given this information, one can review existing student records to determine how he or she currently performs the task.

It is imperative that academic accommodations awarded to students with disabilities are considered in context and are individualized to fit their motor skills, language processing, verbal expression, abstract ability, and sensory functioning (vision, hearing, and tactile). The goal is to choose the simplest accommodation that meets the student's needs. If accommodations are too complex, they may be counterproductive. Ideally, accommodations should be easily available, inexpensive, proven to be effective, portable, and useful for a variety of tasks. Furthermore, the student should be able to learn to use the accommodation in an acceptable timeframe (Beech 2010). Accommodations typically include a change in four general areas, such as how course material is presented and how the student responds to assignments or test questions, scheduling and timing of tests, and test setting.

Proposed Criteria for Accommodations

Beech, Dixon, and Mckay (2013) published a set of general guidelines for the process an IEP team should follow to help select, implement, and evaluate accommodations (Florida Department of Education 2013). The proposed criteria suggest that accommodations of an IEP team should (1) address what is necessary, (2) encourage independence, (3) remain generalizable, and (4) be acceptable. In order for an accommodation to be necessary, it must be required to perform a task, diminish, or remove the effect of the disability, and increase the student's ability to complete a task. Independence criteria is met when the accommodation is easy to use, utilizes the least complex alternative, supports continued skill development, and promotes self-sufficiency. In order for an accommodation to be generalizable, it should be able to be used for similar tasks across different environments. Lastly, an accommodation is considered acceptable when the student is willing to use the accommodation prefers the specific accommodation over others that are effective, and is capable of learning how and knowing when to use the accommodation.

Special Considerations for Selecting and Evaluating Testing Accommodations

When selecting accommodations for the classroom, one should also consider the guidelines for state and district assessments. Students generally use the same types of accommodations in the classroom on such tests; however, certain accommodations may not be used. All states have testing accommodations policies that specify which accommodations, are allowed as well as guidelines for making decisions about testing accommodations. An outline link to any state's accommodation policy can be found at the National Center on Educational Outcomes website (Bolt 2004). In addition, each state has a policy or guideline that specifically says that accommodations used in state testing must be ones used for instruction (Lazarus et al. 2006).

Once accommodations are made and implemented in a student's learning environment, it is critical that their effectiveness is monitored and evaluated. One of the most important factors to measure is the impact on student performance. Specific accommodations can be evaluated by collecting data through interviewing, school observations, and reviewing work samples. While each case must be considered on an individual basis, some suggested accommodations for a variety of disabilities encountered within the classroom setting are described in the following sections.

Reading Disorder

Reading involves two basic components recognized as automaticity and comprehension. Automaticity pertains to the ability to quickly and accurately recognize words, while comprehension refers to the ability to make meaning from words. The combined effect of automaticity and comprehension, labeled as reading fluency, refers to reading quickly, accurately, and with proper prosody to facilitate comprehension (Newhall 2013).

Reading disorder, commonly called dyslexia, is the most common language-based learning disorder. Dyslexia is diagnosed when the student's primary difficulty is automaticity. Many students with reading disorder have an impaired ability to discriminate between morphemes. Such individual's process sounds differently, which inhibits quick and accurate decoding. Other students exhibit trouble reading as a result of disparities in visual processing. Both cases often result in a reduced ability to comprehend and retain written passages, identify relevant themes, learn and employ new vocabulary, and spell words correctly. In addition, such students tend to misperceive similar words and skip phrases due to poor tracking (Newhall 2013).

Reading Tools

Computer programs that can scan textbooks and read course materials are known as text scanners. Some popular text scanners include Kurzwell 3000, WYNN Read, and Write Gold. In addition, digital books have been demonstrated to be very helpful for those with reading disorder (Friedlander 2004). There are multiple areas in which accommodations are suggested for students with reading disorder in a classroom setting; these include: presentation of material, response style, seating, timing and test scheduling, and additional materials.

Presentation of Material

It is suggested that material be presented in small steps, complex information divided into chunks or sections, and important information highlighted or color-coded. Students may utilize books on tape, large print versions of texts, and computer-assisted devices with auditory and visual cues rather than written descriptions. They may be provided background knowledge about particular topics and afforded alternate methods of learning via the incorporation of videotapes or movies or both, which present the same information. The permitted use of tape recorders in class to record lecture material and assignments, graphic organizers (e.g., Venn diagram, story mapping, etc.), and visual aids (overheads, charts, whiteboards, etc.) are equally helpful tools. A peer tutor or note taker may also be assigned.

Response

Students may be offered the opportunity to complete written and oral tests with verbal responses and allowed to dictate their answers to a scribe.

Seating

Preferential seating may be provided and testing may simultaneously be administered in a private room or space with minimal distractions.

Timing and Test Scheduling

Students may receive extended time to complete assignments and tests. Testing may also be administered in multiple-timed sessions or over a period of several days. Frequent breaks are helpful, when necessary.

Additional Materials

Assistive devices that translate text to speech (e.g., text scanners, digital books, screen reader scanner with character recognition software, etc.) and a specialized tilt-top desk or bookstand to hold materials for easier reading as well as any optical enhancer (e.g., magnifier) are suggested supplementary tools. Other suggested aids include: a list of relevant vocabulary words with definitions, chapter outlines or study guides that highlight main themes in assigned course work, and the use of templates to block out parts of the text in order to focus on particular words. Students should be provided with alternative resources that contain similar content at a lower reading level.

Spoken Language Disorder

Students with a spoken language disorder demonstrate impairment in the acquisition and use of language due to deficits across one or more language domains, which include the understanding of speech sounds and rules (phonology), the smallest units of meaning in words (morphology), word order and sentence structure (syntax), vocabulary knowledge (semantics), and use of language appropriately in social situations (pragmatics) (American Speech-Language-Hearing Association 2016). Similar to reading disorder suggestions, there are many areas in which accommodations may be made for students with both expressive and receptive spoken language disorder in a classroom setting.

Presentation of Material

Receptive: It is suggested that material be presented in small steps and complex information divided into chunks or sections. Students may be provided background knowledge about particular topics and given alternate methods of learning by means of videotapes or movies or both to present course material. They may also be allowed to use audiotaped texts and other readings, graphic organizers (e.g., Venn diagram, story mapping, etc.), and visual aids (overheads, charts, and whiteboards) to connect ideas. Students would benefit from the use of interactive CDs or have access to computer-assisted training with auditory and visual cues rather than written descriptions.

Receptive and Expressive: Advanced warning may be given before calling on a student, reading and writing may be divided into steps, and a peer tutor or note taker may be assigned.

Response

Receptive: Alternate assignments may be made available to students; these alternatives should address similar content at a lower reading level. Students may also be allowed to complete written and oral tests with verbal responses.

Receptive and Expressive: The question-answer formatting for class-work, quizzes, and tests may be multiple-choice, true or false, or match-ing. Additionally, it is useful to reduce the overall amount of questions on assignments and worksheets.

Seating

Receptive and Expressive: Preferential seating may be provided and test-ing administered in a private room or space with minimal distractions.

Timing and Test Scheduling

Receptive and Expressive: Students may receive extended time to respond to questions, and complete assignments and tests or both. Testing may also be administered in multiple-timed sessions or over a period of several days. Frequent breaks may be offered and allowed.

Additional Materials

Receptive: A specialized tilt-top desk or bookstand to hold materials for easier reading is a suggested tool, as well as any optical enhancer (e.g., magnifier).

Receptive and Expressive: Students may be allowed to use headphones for tape recorders and assistive devices that translate text to speech (e.g., reading pens, Kurzweil 3000, character recognition software). They may also be granted access to chapter outlines or teacher notes or both, to provide context to deduce meaning and highlight main themes in assigned coursework. A list of relevant vocabulary words that contain specific definitions is also suggested.

Written Disorder

Writing ability involves fine motor skills, spelling ability, and intact expressive language. Impairment in any of these processes may lead to problems with written expression (Newhall 2013). In particular, difficulty with any part of language (phonemes, morphemes, syntax, etc.) can inhibit the development of writing ability. Students with specific learning disorders in writing demonstrate difficulty with sentence structure and organization of writing, which results in disorganized sentences, disordered argument or plot, grammatical errors, spelling and capitalization mistakes, trouble with letters, speech sound substitutions, and poor penmanship.

Multimedia Tools

Multimedia applications allow students to use text, pictures, movies, graphics, and sound together in a presentation or project. These programs allow students to demonstrate their knowledge by utilizing multiple abilities in creative ways. Furthermore, such tools help create an engaging classroom environment. A few examples of popular multimedia tools include PowerPoint, iMovie, HyperStudio, MediaBlender, and mPower (Friedlander 2004). Suggested accommodations and modifications for students with a specific learning disorder in writing is described in the following sections.

Presentation of Material

As previously suggested, it is helpful when the material is presented in small steps with complex information divided into chunks or sections.

Tape-recorded lectures are also suggested in classroom settings, along with structured outlines and graphic organizers (e.g., Venn diagram, story mapping, etc.) to plan writing. Students may be assigned a peer tutor or in-class note taker.

Response

A student may submit or respond to classroom assignments and tests in various ways, such as transcription, orally, and via audiotaped responses. Multimedia tools may also be used with the different response styles. Keyword responses are acceptable instead of complete sentences and spelling errors are permissible.

Seating

Similar to previous mentioned seating accommodations, preferential seating ought be provided and testing administered in a private room or space to reduce the chance of external noises and distractions.

Timing and Test Scheduling

Timing may be extended for completion of tests, quizzes, and written assignments. Furthermore, testing sessions may be scheduled in a manner that allows a student ample opportunity to complete them successfully (i.e., tests administered in several timed sessions or over several days). It is also recommended that students be allowed frequent breaks during assignments and tests.

Additional Materials

Students may be allowed to use laptop computers or some form of word processor on assignments and tests. Further, special word processing software that anticipates a student's writing, a transcriber for hand-written coursework, and planning software for writing assignments is suggested. Two copies of worksheets or tests may be provided, which would allow the student to work on one as a draft and then use the other as a final copy. The use of a thesaurus, outlining, and brainstorming are also recommended as methods to aid the student in finding and planning words to write or say. The use of graph paper for writing is suggested to help the student organize information and align numbers in computation problems. Other supplementary suggestions include: worksheets and tests with ample space for writing answers, text-to-speech or voice output systems, spelling dictionaries or electronic spelling aids with speech capabilities, structured outlines or graphic organizers to plan written assignments, and adaptive devices (e.g., pencil grips, special pens or pencil holders, erasable pens, or special paper with raised or color-coded line indicators).

Mathematics Disorder

Students with specific learning disorders in mathematics have difficulty in understanding basic mathematical facts, concepts, and processes, resulting in poor comprehension and computation. Such students demonstrate an impaired ability to memorize math facts, calculate arithmetic problems fluently and accurately, and use mathematical reasoning. Further, they tend to confuse operational signals, order of operations, and have limited understanding of ratios, proportions, and relative size.

It is important to note that many math problems require more than calculation ability and number sense. Several mathematical procedures also depend upon oral and written language skills (Newhall 2013). Similar to former suggestions, there are numerous methods in which accommodations and modifications can be made for students with math disorders.

Presentation of Material

It is suggested that a flowchart be used to display and label steps for solving multistep problems. Students should be permitted to use graph paper or color coding as a means to organize math problems, their keywords, and their corresponding answers (e.g., colored pencils or highlighters). Students may also complete shorter assignments that measure the same objective as lengthier coursework. It is recommended that sample math problems remain on the board during the presentation of new material. Peer assistance and tutoring opportunities may be arranged.

Seating

Preferential seating should be provided and testing should be administered in a private room or space as a means to limit distractions.

Timing and Test Scheduling

Students should receive extended time to complete assignments and tests. Testing may also be administered in multiple-timed sessions or over a period of several days. Frequent breaks should be allowed during testing, when necessary.

Additional Materials

Students may use graph paper for writing to aid in organizing information and in the alignment of numbers within computation problems. They may also use tables with math facts (e.g., multiplication table, etc.) and diagrams on tests.

Deaf and the Hearing Impaired

Students with hearing impairment represent a heterogeneous group who exhibit a range of difficulties with classroom instruction and specific types of assignments and exams. While some students with hearing loss are able to speak, there is variability in the fluency of their voices. Hearing loss has a direct effect on specific capacities pertaining to vocal control, pronunciation, and volume that impact the ability to monitor their voice and verbally express ideas. Many students with hearing impairment are delayed in language resulting in reduced comprehension of written materials and poor writing ability. Such students often depend on visual cues for assistance and use lip-reading and hearing aids to communicate. Students with hearing loss may also benefit from auditory trainers, such as "magnetic induction loops, infrared light systems, or frequency-modulated radio frequency systems that enhance favorable signal-to-noise ratio" (Lukomski 2004). In these cases, the teacher is given a microphone that is connected to the hearing aid, which helps such students hear the teacher. Suggested accommodations for students with hearing impairment can be found as follows.

Presentation of Material

Students tend to benefit from material that is presented visually, submitting assignments in written form, and when visual media is used as supplemental instruction to what is being taught. The use of an interpreter should be allowed, along with usage of a tape recorder for class lectures. A peer tutor may be assigned and an in-class note taker designated.

Seating

Preferential seating should be provided.

Timing

Timing may be extended for completion of assignments and tests.

Additional Materials

Students and interpreters may be provided with a recorded list of technical terminology and unfamiliar words and terms along with a list of relevant vocabulary words and definitions. They may also benefit from access to chapter outlines or study guides that highlight main themes in assigned coursework. Amplified hearing devices or word processing devices (e.g., AlphaSmart, communication boards, and other augmentative devices) are allowable.

Blind or the Visually Impaired

A visual impairment is any visual condition that impacts an individual's ability to effectively perform activities of daily living. Students with visual impairments experience impairments of the visual system that impact their ability to learn. Students may qualify for special education services if their total or partial vision loss interferes with their academic performance (Morgan and Klar 2004). Visual impairment is classified into three categories according to an individual's level of functional vision:

1. Low vision: Students use their vision as their primary sensory channel.
2. Functionally blind: Students can use limited vision for functional tasks but need their tactile and auditory channels for learning.
3. Totally blind: Students use tactile and auditory channels for learning and functional tasks.

An additional classification system is also used to differentiate congenital (occurs during fetal development or immediately following birth) from adventitious (occurs after having normal vision) causes. It is important to note that students with congenital visual impairment typically have more difficulty mastering visually strengthened concepts such as spatial orientation and many environmental concepts (Texas Council for Developmental Disabilities 2013).

Software Solutions

Certain software programs allow students with visual impairment to perform basic mathematical operations and show their work. Programs for more advanced mathematics include Scientific Notebook, LiveMath, and Geometer's Sketchpad. Other software programs, known as screen readers, assist students with visual impairment by reading screen icons, text, and other content on the computer monitor. ZoomText and Jaws are two popular Windows programs that allow the student to enlarge the screen and text (Friedlander 2004). With the help of these programs, students with visual impairment gain access to word documents, other helpful programs and tools, and the Internet. In addition to screen readers, text scanners and digital books may also be appropriate for students with visual impairment. A number of suggested accommodations for students with visual impairments are described as follows.

Presentation of Material

It is suggested that students benefit from the utilization of Braille text-books and materials, books on tape, and computer-assisted devices with auditory cues rather than written descriptions, as well as the incorporation of audiotapes that present the same information. Students may receive verbal directions for assignments and tests. Further, the use of tape-recorded syllabuses, lecture notes, and other relevant coursework may also be beneficial. Other helpful tools include: providing textbook titles in advance so that taped copies can be made, highlighting or color coding of important information on handouts, and the assignment of a peer tutor or note taker.

Response

Students may be offered the opportunity to complete written and oral tests with verbal responses and allowed to dictate their answers to a scribe. They may also be allowed to submit tape recordings of written assignments and tests.

Seating

Preferential seating may be provided. It is permissible for students to move around the room as needed to see information that is being presented away from their desk. Adjusting light intensity in the room may also be helpful, along with the use of artificial lighting when brightness levels become low in the classroom.

Timing and Test Scheduling

Students may receive extended time to complete assignments and tests. Testing may also be administered in multiple-timed sessions or over a period of several days. Frequent breaks are also helpful.

Additional Materials

The use of raised lined paper, recordings of relevant vocabulary words with definitions, portable note takers that electronically receive, store, and retrieve data and are equipped with speech or refreshable Braille display output are suggested supplementary tools. The use of optical enhancers (e.g., magnifier), other visual aids, and software programs that allow students to compute math with their work shown and listen to book chapters or assignments may also be helpful. Students also tend to benefit from having access to audio-recorded chapter outlines or study guides that highlight main themes in assigned coursework.

Nonverbal Learning Disorder

Nonverbal learning disorders (NVLD) affect student's academic progress, as well as social and emotional development. Students with NVLD have an impaired ability to connect visual information with abstract concepts, organize the spatial relationships of input from their visual field, adapt to novel situations, or accurately read nonverbal signs and cues. Such students process information at a slow rate, which causes difficulty performing tasks that involve speed and flexibility (Thompson 1996). In addition to these impaired abilities, students with NVLD may struggle with arithmetic, particularly complex math that involves multiple columns (e.g., long division), word problems, and problems that rely on spatial abilities and relationship between concepts. In some cases, students have adequate language skills, but they have trouble in organizing information, understanding abstract concepts, and may miss nonverbal cues. Furthermore, students with NVLD may demonstrate reduced coordination in both fine and gross motor skills, and balance (Spina Bifida Family Support 2006). Suggested accommodations to help students overcome the difficulties associated with visual impairments can be found as follows.

Presentation of Material

Students tend to benefit from the presentation of materials in verbal form with the incorporation of rich descriptions. Limited use of paper and pencil tasks may also be advantageous. Students may be provided with background knowledge about particular topics, as well as recorded lists that contain instructions for assignments. Simplifying test answer-sheet layouts and the arrangement of visual-spatial assignments may be permitted.

Response

Students may be allowed the use of a laptop computer or word processor for all written assignments and test.

Seating

Preferential seating may be provided.

Timing and Test Scheduling

Students may receive extended time to complete assignments and tests. Testing may also be administered in multiple-timed sessions or over a period of several days. Frequent breaks are allowable.

Additional Materials

Granting access to chapter outlines or study guides that highlight main themes in assigned coursework is suggested. Supplementing lined paper with graph paper for written math assignments and other coursework may also be beneficial.

Motor Impairment

Motor impairment is characterized by partial or complete loss of functioning as a result of a spinal cord injury, amputation, or musculoskeletal back disorder (St. Petersberg College 2007). Students with motor impairment may experience involuntary movement, total paralysis, and decreased levels of function in tasks that require fine and gross motor skills, and balance. Such students may exhibit impaired coordination, slow motor movements, as well as motor weakness in both upper and lower body posture. Suggested accommodations that may help students with motor impairment are detailed as follows.

Presentation of Material

Students may be assigned a peer tutor or note taker. They may also benefit from tape-recorded syllabuses, lecture notes, and other relevant coursework.

Response

The opportunity to complete written and oral tests with verbal responses is helpful. Students may also be allowed to dictate their answers to a scribe and submit tape recordings of written assignments and tests.

Seating

Preferential seating may be provided.

Timing and Test Scheduling

As mentioned previously, students may receive extended time to complete assignments and tests. Testing may also be administered in multiple-timed sessions or over a period of several days. Frequent breaks may be given.

Additional Materials

Providing a recording of relevant vocabulary words with definitions and allowing the use of voice-activated assistive technology will help students perform assignments. Students will also benefit from having access to audio-recorded chapter outlines or study guides that highlight main themes in assigned coursework.

CHAPTER 5

Case Studies

Reading Disorder—John, 18 Years Old

John's parents indicated that during early elementary his teachers reported he had significant difficulty with reading and comprehension. His parents explained he also struggled with expressing his thoughts on paper when prompted to create narratives regarding stories he had read in class or even free writing responses. In addition to his difficulties with translating his thoughts on paper, he also experienced issues with grasping spelling, grammar, punctuation, structuring sentences properly, and replacing pronouns with incorrect words such as "the" instead of "she." He was retained in fourth grade for not passing the state mandated reading assessment. At this time, he received supplemental aid courses and was placed on an Individual Education Plan (IEP) to aid him in his difficulties with reading ability, reading comprehension, test taking, writing ability, and focusing. While on IEP, John received accommodations including twice the allotted time allowed on tests, small group testing, and preferential seating. During the time period in which he received academic accommodations, he had variable success in different courses often receiving As, Bs, Cs, and Ds. According to his records, the majority of the Cs and Ds he attained were in his English courses.

For his sixth through eighth grades years, he was transferred to a private junior high school where he was not awarded any of the aforementioned accommodations during this time; however, the school consisted of smaller classes with roughly 15 to 16 students in each class. John, as well as his parents, reported that the smaller number of students allowed him to have more one-on-one instruction with his teachers. Despite this, John expressed that he still struggled with being able to read the required texts efficiently during school and outside.

John attended a different private school for ninth grade and his grades continued to drop. He became quite frustrated when required to read aloud at school, write about his thoughts on a particular story, or answer essay or short answer questions regarding aspects of a narrative. John expressed having difficulty organizing his thoughts in order to create a cohesive answer on paper. In addition, he described remembering particular aspects of the story to be challenging when required to answer questions regarding the text. His difficulty with understanding questions regarding a story and organizing his thoughts often causes him to either rush through a test and make careless mistakes or take too much time on any one question, which causes him to blindly answer questions in order to finish on time.

Test Results for John

Wechsler Adult Intelligence Scale, Fourth Edition

The Wechsler Adult Intelligence Scale, Fourth Edition (WAIS-IV) is a measure of general intellectual functioning.

Verbal Comprehension Index	Score	Perceptual Reasoning Index	Score
Similarities	10	Block Design	10
Vocabulary	9	Matrix Reasoning	11
Information	9	Visual Puzzles	11
Working Memory Index	**Score**	**Processing Speed Index**	**Score**
Digit Span	9	Symbol Search	9
Arithmetic	8	Coding	10
Index Scores	**Score**		
Full Scale IQ	97		
Verbal Comprehension	96		
Perceptual Reasoning	104		
Working Memory	92		
Processing Speed	97		

Wechsler Memory Scale, Fourth Edition

The Wechsler Memory Scale, Fourth Edition (WMS-IV) is a test of an individual's visual and verbal memory functioning.

Subtests	Score	Subtests	Score
Logical Memory I	10	Logical Memory II	10
Designs I	11	Designs II	11
Verbal Paired Associates I	11	Verbal Paired Associates II	12
Visual Reproduction I	12	Visual Reproduction II	14
Index Scores	**Score**		
Auditory Memory	104		
Visual Memory	112		
Immediate Memory	107		
Delayed Memory	112		

Woodcock-Johnson Cognitive, Third Edition

The Woodcock-Johnson Cognitive, Third Edition (WJC-III) COG is a test that assesses many aspects of cognitive functioning, including visual spatial thinking, auditory processing, fluid reasoning, and processing speed.

Clusters	Standard Score	Subtest	Standard Score
General Intellectual Ability	91	Verbal Comprehension	91
Verbal Ability	95	Visual-Auditory Learn	108
Thinking Ability	101	Spatial Relations	105
Cognitive Efficiency	92	Sound Blending	93
Phonemic Awareness	97	Concept Formation	98
Working Memory	95	Visual Matching	92
Delayed Recall	107	Numbers Reversed	97
		Incomplete Words	104
		Aud. Work Memory	93
		Vis-Aud Learn Delayed	109

Woodcock-Johnson Tests of Achievement, Third Edition

The Woodcock-Johnson Tests of Achievement, Third Edition is an extensive test of academic achievement in a variety of areas, including tests involving word identification, fluency, and comprehension as well as mathematical calculations and fluency, and spelling and writing fluency.

Clusters	Standard Score	Subtest	Standard Score
Total Achievement	84	Letter-Word Identification	83
Oral Language	89	Reading Fluency	74
Broad Math	94	Story Recall	106
Broad Written Language	94	Understanding Directions	95
Broad Reading	81	Calculation	99
Brief Reading	84	Math Fluency	99
Brief Math	98	Spelling	91
Math Calculation Skills	91	Writing Fluency	93
Brief Writing	92	Passage Comprehension	89
Written Expression	93	Applied Problems	98
Academic Fluency	82	Writing Samples	92
Academic Applications	92	Story Recall Delayed	102
Academic Skill	87		

Nelson Denny Reading Test

The Nelson Denny Reading Test (NDRT) is an assessment of an individual's ability in three areas of academic achievement: vocabulary, reading comprehension, and reading rate. Both the standard time administration (15-minute vocabulary, 20-minute comprehension) and extended time (24-minute vocabulary, 32-minute comprehension) administration portions were given.

Standard Administration			
Test	Raw	Standard Score	Grade Equivalent
Vocabulary	28	83	7.9
Comprehension	14	69	4.1
Reading Rate	106	71	-
Total	42	74	5.1

Extended Administration			
Test	Raw	Standard Score	Grade Equivalent
Vocabulary	35	92	9.6
Comprehension	26	84	7.1
Total	61	87	8.3

Peabody Picture Vocabulary Test, Fourth Edition

The Peabody Picture Vocabulary Test, Fourth Edition (PPVT-4) is a measure of receptive (hearing) vocabulary, which is used to assess one's verbal ability. The examinee is shown several different pictures of scenes or objects and is asked to point to the picture that represents the word given verbally. John's performance on this task fell at the low end of the average range. Standard scores from 85 to 115 are considered average. Complete scores are listed as follows.

Raw Score	Standard Score	Age Equivalent	Grade Equivalent
189	93	15:7	10:0

Expressive Vocabulary Test, Second Edition

The Expressive Vocabulary Test, Second Edition (EVT-2) measures expressive (spoken) vocabulary and word retrieval ability. The examinee is shown various scenes or objects and is asked to respond using a single word to questions about a label for a picture, what is going on in a scene, or provide a synonym for a word that fits the context of a scene. John's scores fell in the low end of the average range. Standard scores from 85 to 115 are considered average. Complete scores are listed as follows.

Raw Score	Standard Score	Age Equivalent	Grade Equivalent
131	86	12:9	7:3

Conners Continuous Performance Test-III

The Conners Continuous Performance Test-III (CPT-III) is a computerized visual performance test that examines sustained attention and impulse control. John's performance fell within normal limits. T-scores above 70 are indicative of possible impairment. Complete scores are listed below.

Measure	T-Score
Detectability	54
Omissions	59
Commissions	58
Perseverations	45
Hit Reaction Time	42
Hit Reaction Time Standard Deviation	42
Variability	45
Hit Reaction Time Block Change	56
Hit Reaction Time Interstimulus Interval Change	48

Conners Continuous Auditory Test of Attention

The Conners Continuous Auditory Test of Attention (CATA) is a computerized auditory performance test that assesses auditory processing and attention. John's performance was within normal limits.

Measure	T-Score
Detectability	50
Omissions	49
Commissions	46
Perseverations	48
Hit Reaction Time	40
Hit Reaction Time Standard Deviation	48
Hit Reaction Time Block Change	54
Level of Attention Deficits	None
Response Pattern	None
Auditory Laterality	No Advantage

Wisconsin Card Sorting Test

The Wisconsin Card Sorting Test (WCST) is used to assess executive functioning, namely the ability to shift and maintain problem-solving strategies for abstract problems when given feedback. A computerized 128-card version of the test was used for this evaluation. John's overall scores fell within expected levels. Complete scores are listed as follows.

Measure	Raw	T-Score
Total Categories Completed	6	
Number of Trials to Complete First Category	14	
Total Number Correct	71	
Total Percent Correct	81	
Total Number Errors	17	55
Total Percent Errors	19	53
Total Number Perseverative Responses	7	60
Total Number Perseverative Errors	7	59
Total Percent Perseverative Errors	8	58
Total Number Nonperseverative Errors	10	51
Total Number Other Responses	0	
Percent Conceptual Level Response	77	53
Total of Failure to Maintain Sets	1	
Learning to Learn Score	0.95	

Category Test

The Category Test is a computerized evaluative tool used to measure non-verbal concept formation and the ability to shift and maintain problem-solving strategies. John's score fell within normal limits. Complete scores are listed below.

Number of Errors	Heaton SS	T-Score
17	13	60

Conners 3 Rating Scales

Parent Form

The Conners 3 Parent Rating Scale provides information about a child's behavior from a parent's point of view.

Scale	Mother	Father
	T-Score	T-Score
Inattention	89	72
Hyperactivity or Impulsivity	54	45
Learning Problems	97	95
Executive Functioning	68	68
Aggression	53	43
Peer Relations	41	60
Global Index Total	59	47
DSM-IV Inattentive	84	74
DSM-IV Hyperactivity or Impulsivity	48	45
DSM-IV Conduct Disorder	48	44
DSM-IV Oppositional Defiant Disorder	44	41

Validity Scales	Raw Score	Cut-Off Score	Raw Score	Cut-Off Score
Positive Impression	1	≥4	0	≥4
Negative Impression	1	≥3	0	≥3
Inconsistency Index	5	≥6	4	≥6
Symptom Counts				
Inattentive ADHD Symptoms	7	≥6	6	≥6
Hyperactive or Impulsive ADHD Symptoms	1	≥6	0	≥6
Conduct Disorder Symptoms	0	≥3	0	≥3
Oppositional Defiant Disorder Symptoms	0	≥4	0	≥4
Functional Impairment				
Schoolwork or Grades	3	3 = Sig. Impairment	3	3 = Sig. Impairment
Friendships or Relationships	0	3 = Sig. Impairment	0	3 = Sig. Impairment
Home Life	0	3 = Sig. Impairment	0	3 = Sig. Impairment
Conners ADHD Probability Percentage	87		64	

Teacher Form

The Conners 3 Teacher Rating Scale provides information about a child's behavior from a teacher's point of view.

Scale	Spanish T-Score	Ethics T-Score	Chemistry T-Score	Algebra T-Score	History T-Score
Inattention	72	72	95	49	45
Hyperactivity or Impulsivity	45	43	43	49	45
Learning Problems	63	89	102	50	47
Executive Functioning	56	68	75	49	47
Aggression	49	44	49	47	44
Peer Relations	70	51	51	51	51
Global Index Total	57	48	59	54	45
DSM-IV Inattentive	80	82	104	57	48
DSM-IV Hyperactivity or Impulsivity	46	43	43	51	46
DSM-IV Conduct Disorder	55	43	49	43	43
DSM-IV Oppositional Defiant Disorder	44	44	49	49	44

Validity Scales	Raw Score	Raw Score	Raw Score	Raw Score	Raw Score	Cut-Off Score
Positive Impression	0	0	1	0	0	≥4
Negative Impression	3	1	3	2	0	≥3
Inconsistency Index	4	4	1	2	3	≥6
Symptom Counts						
Inattentive ADHD Symptoms	7	8	9	0	0	≥6
Hyperactive or Impulsive ADHD Symptoms	0	0	0	1	0	≥6
Conduct Disorder Symptoms	1	0	0	0	0	≥3
Oppositional Defiant Disorder Symptoms	0	0	1	1	0	≥4

(Continued)

(Continued)

Functional Impairment						
Schoolwork or Grades	3	3	3	1	0	3 = Sig. Impairment
Friendships or Relationships	2	1	2	0	0	3 = Sig. Impairment
Conners ADHD Probability Percentage	77	77	92	19	39	

Personality Inventory for Children, Second Edition

The Personality Inventory for Children, Second Edition (PIC-2) is an objective measure used for child personality assessment.

The client's father's scores are listed below.

Scale	T-Score	Scale	T-Score
INC (Inconsistency)	44	RLT (Reality Distortion)	45
FB (Dissimulation)	46	Rlt1 (Developmental Deviate)	42
DEF (Defensiveness)	54	Rlt2 (Hallucination or Delusion)	50
COG (Cognitive Impairment)	60	SOM (Somatic Concern)	62
Cog1 (Inadequate Abilities)	60	Som1 (Psychosomatic)	73
Cog2 (Poor Achievement)	66	Som2 (Muscle Tension or Anxiety)	42
Cog3 (Developmental Delay)	43	DIS (Psychological Discomfort)	42
ADH (Impulsivity or Distractible)	57	Dis1 (Fear or Worry)	38
Adh1 (Disruptive Behavior)	57	Dis2 (Depression)	46
Adh2 (Fearlessness)	56	Dis3 (Sleep or Death Concern)	45
DLQ (Delinquency)	48	WDL (Social Withdrawal)	46
Dlq1 (Antisocial)	54	Wdl1 (Social Introversion)	45
Dlq2 (Dyscontrol)	46	Wdl2 (Isolation)	50
Dlq3 (Noncompliance)	48	SSK (Social Skill Deficits)	49
FAM (Family Dysfunction)	44	Ssk1 (Limited Peer Status)	54
Fam1 (Member Conflicts)	42	Ssk2 (Conflict with Peers)	43
Fam2 (Parent Maladjustment)	49		

The client's mother's scores are listed below.

Scale	T-Score	Scale	T-Score
INC (Inconsistency)	49	RLT (Reality Distortion)	47
FB (Dissumulation)	43	Rlt1 (Developmental Deviate)	46
DEF (Defensiveness)	54	Rlt2 (Hallucination or Delusion)	50
COG (Cognitive Impairment)	66	SOM (Somatic Concern)	52
Cog1 (Inadequate Abilities)	68	Som1 (Psychosomatic)	53
Cog2 (Poor Achievement)	66	Som2 (Muscle tension or Anxiety)	50
Cog3 (Developmental Delay)	49	DIS (Psychological Discomfort)	50
ADH (Impulsivity or Distractible)	55	Dis1 (Fear or Worry)	54
Adh1 (Disruptive Behavior)	51	Dis2 (Depression)	49
Adh2 (Fearlessness)	65	Dis3 (Sleep or Death Concern)	45
DLQ (Delinquency)	45	WDL (Social Withdrawal)	50
Dlq1 (Antisocial)	46	Wdl1 (Social Introversion)	49
Dlq2 (Dyscontrol)	46	Wdl2 (Isolation)	50
Dlq3 (Noncompliance)	46	SSK (Social Skill Deficits)	43
FAM (Family Dysfunction)	41	Ssk1 (Limited Peer Status)	45
Fam1 (Member Conflicts)	42	Ssk2 (Conflict with Peers)	43
Fam2 (Parent Maladjustment)	43		

Test of Memory Malingering

The Test of Memory Malingering (TOMM) is used to assess the degree of effort displayed by a client on memory tasks. John scored in the normal range on this test. Trial 2 or Retention scores below 45 are considered questionable. Complete scores are listed below.

Trial	Score
Trial 1	50
Trial 2	50
Retention Trial	50

Summary of Test Results

Neuropsychological testing revealed John's overall level of intellectual functioning to be in the average range, with no significant discrepancies between his verbal, nonverbal, working memory, and processing speed abilities. His auditory and immediate memory abilities fell within the average range and his visual and delayed memory abilities were in the high average range. There were no significant differences between his ability to recall information, whether it was presented in a visual or oral manner. There were also no discrepancies in his ability to recall information immediately or after a delay. On a measure of cognitive functioning, including visual spatial thinking, auditory processing, fluid reasoning, and processing speed (Woodcock Johnson Cognitive, Third Edition. WCJIII-COG), his scores were also all within the average range, consistent with his measured intellectual abilities on the WAIS-IV.

An extensive test of John's academic achievement in a variety of areas, including tests involving word identification, fluency, and comprehension as well as mathematical calculations and fluency, and spelling and writing fluency (Woodcock Johnson Achievement, Third Edition WCJ-III-ACH), is the measure that started to show where John's difficulties were. When looking at the scores, he falls in the average range in most areas, in math, both timed and untimed, spelling, and writing. However, when looking at his reading abilities, you will see he performs in the below average (1.5 standard deviations below intellectual abilities) range on a speeded measure of reading fluency. On an untimed reading measure (Passage Comprehension), he is able to perform at expected levels. On another test of speeded reading ability (NDRT), John performs in the impaired range when asked to answer questions about complex narrative passages. He also has a slow reading rate. When he was provided with 60 percent extra time, his ability to perform on a timed comprehension task increased to the low average range, a significant improvement. Testing also showed that he has some difficulty with receptive language, scoring in the below average range, but his receptive language was within expected levels.

John's parents and teachers had concerns about his attention and concentration and these concerns were evident on parent rating forms. Both parents reported that he experiences significant learning problems such as failing to understand what he reads, difficulty spelling words, needing additional explanation of instructions, and failing to understand the big picture of things. Additionally, both of his parents indicated that he is strongly inattentive to details, has difficulty following through on instructions, organizing tasks, and frequently loses things. His Spanish II, Ethics, and Chemistry teachers endorsed items indicating problems with inattention and problems with completing and understanding schoolwork and low grades. John's Spanish II teacher reported that he sometimes appears to be unaccepted by his peers, occasionally interacts with others, and has poor social skills whereas his other teachers did not report this. Furthermore, his Ethics and Chemistry teachers responded to items indicating significant learning difficulties such as having difficulty remembering what he reads, trouble reading, does not understand what he is reading, and forgets things easily. These teachers also reported that he has difficulty starting tasks, trouble deciding what things are most important, failing to finish things he has already started, and forgetting to turn in completed work. Therefore, measures of sustained attention were given. Scores on the CPT-III, measuring visual sustained attention do not show any evidence of difficulties and neither did a measure of sustained auditory attention (CATA). With regards to executive functioning, John scored with the Average range on all measures and no deficits were exhibited.

On an objective measure of child personality assessment (PIC-2), John's father indicated that John experienced a high number of somatic complaints, including being easily fatigued, having headaches and backaches, and an overall tendency toward exaggeration in terms of his physical health. His mother did not endorse any items that reached a significant level.

Diagnosis

Based on the reported history and records provided, a diagnosis of specific learning disorder, with impairment in reading was considered. This disorder involves difficulty learning and using academic skills, despite the provision of interventions that target the specific difficulties. The difficulties must have persisted for at least 6 months. This disturbance also is substantially below the expected level given the client's chronological age, and causes significant interference with academic or occupational performance or with activities of daily living, as confirmed by individually administered standardized achievement measures and comprehensive clinical assessment. This disturbance also interferes with academic achievement and cannot be due to a medical condition. Signs associated with a specific learning disorder with impairment in reading include difficulty in word reading accuracy, reading rate or fluency, and reading comprehension. The learning difficulties begin during school-age years but may not become fully manifest until the demands for those affected academic skills exceed the individual's limited capacities. The learning difficulties are not better accounted for by intellectual disabilities, uncorrected visual or auditory actuary, other mental or neurological disorders, psychosocial adversity, lack of proficiency in the language of academic instruction, or inadequate educational instruction.

According to report from John, his mother, and father, and a review of his records, there is an extended history of reading and reading comprehension problems. His mother reported that the challenges he experiences came to her attention when he was in third grade. She further explained that as the material focused on in school became more demanding for John, his difficulty in understanding complex sentence structure, underlying themes of stories, recalling words, and slow reading ability became more apparent. Both of his parents agreed that these difficulties influenced their decision to place him in the public school system so that he would be able to receive proper academic accommodations. He was retained in the fourth grade due to failing the standardized achievement testing in reading required by the state. His parents reported that while receiving accommodations he attained As, Bs, and Cs. Upon transferring to a private school and losing his accommodations, John exhibited difficulties in areas pertaining to reading and comprehension and his grades dropped to Ds or Fs in reading and English courses.

Results of the neuropsychological evaluation suggest that John has difficulties in timed reading and passage comprehension. When compared to his overall Full Scale Intelligence Quotient (FSIQ) score of 97 on the WAIS-IV, his comprehension score of 69 on the NDRT fell 1.5 standard deviations below his IQ, suggesting a significant discrepancy between his current reading ability and measured intellectual ability. On the Woodcock-Johnson Tests of Achievement, Third Edition, John's reading fluency (Standard Score = 74) fell significantly below expected levels while his ability to perform reading comprehension tasks under untimed conditions fell within expected levels (letter-word = 83; passage comprehension = 89). Based on these results, John meets criteria for a specific learning disorder, with impairment in reading.

Specific Learning Disorder, with Impairment in Written Expression—Charlie, 14 Years Old

Charlie, a 14-year-old Hispanic male, was referred for updated testing due to academic difficulties. Charlie's mother described that he has struggled to maintain a proper developmental trajectory in comparison to his peers. She noted that he was slow to learn language and did not begin speaking until he was approximately 3 years old.

Elementary school records indicate that he received Bs and Cs primarily in his math and science courses, but attained Cs, Ds, and Fs in his reading and language arts and was required to repeat the third grade due to not passing state mandated testing. During that year, he achieved Cs and Bs in his reading and language arts courses and As and Cs in his math and science courses. His records indicate that he was administratively promoted to the fourth grade and continued to obtain Bs, Cs, and Ds in all of his core classes (i.e., math, reading, science, social studies, etc.) for his fourth and fifth grades years. During his sixth grade year he received primarily Ds in his language arts courses and Cs in his math and science classes.

At the age of 12, based on school testing, Charlie was placed on an IEP to help him with his difficulties in writing ability. While on IEP, he received accommodations within the classroom as well as state mandated testing (e.g., additional time, oral rather than written responses, dictation of answers on essays, frequent breaks, and small group for testing).

Test Results

Wechsler Intelligence Scale for Children, Fourth Edition

The Wechsler Intelligence Scale for Children, Fourth Edition (WISC-IV) is a measure of general intellectual functioning.

Verbal Comprehension Subtests	Score	Visual Spatial Subtests	Score
Vocabulary	12	Block Design	7
Similarities	15	Visual Puzzles	11
Working Memory Subtests	**Score**	**Processing Speed Subtests**	**Score**
Digit Span	9	Coding	9
Picture Span	10	Symbol Search	12
Fluid Reasoning		**Score**	
Matrix Reasoning		10	
Figure Weights		10	
Index Scores		**Score**	
Full Scale IQ		102	
Verbal Comprehension		118	
Visual Spatial		94	
Fluid Reasoning		100	
Working Memory		97	
Processing Speed		103	

Wide Range Assessment of Memory and Learning, Second Edition

The Wide Range Assessment of Memory and Learning, Second Edition (WRAML-2) is used to assess memory function.

Core Subtests	Scaled Score	Recognition Subtests	Scaled Score
Story Memory	14	Story Recognition	10
Design Memory	10	Design Recognition	10
Verbal Learning	11	Verbal Learning Recognition	12
Picture Memory	8	Picture Memory Recognition	9
Finger Windows	9		
Number-Letter	9		
Delay Recall Subtests		**Scaled Score**	
Story Memory Recall		12	
Verbal Learning Recall		11	

Index scores	Standard Score
General Memory	101
Verbal Memory	114
Visual Memory	94
Attention or Concentration	94
Verbal Recognition	96
Visual Recognition	106
General Recognition	101

Wechsler Individual Achievement Test, Third Edition

The Wechsler Individual Achievement Test, Third Edition (WIAT-III) is an extensive test of academic achievement in a variety of areas, including tests involving word identification, fluency and comprehension as well as mathematical calculations and fluency, and spelling and writing fluency.

Subtest	Standard Score
Listening Comprehension	96
Receptive Vocabulary	101
Oral Discourse Comprehension	93
Reading Comprehension	102
Math Problem-Solving	94
Sentence Composition	108
Sentence Combining	116
Sentence Building	99
Word Reading	115
Essay Paragraph Composition	69
Word Count	51
Theme Development and Text Organization	86
Pseudoword Decoding	103
Numerical Operations	101
Oral Reading Fluency	110
Oral Reading Accuracy	118
Oral Reading Rate	107
Spelling	100

(Continued)

(Continued)

Math Fluency-Addition	120
Math Fluency-Subtraction	108
Math Fluency-Multiplication	131
Composite and Total Scores	
Total Reading	109
Basic Reading	108
Reading Comprehension and Fluency	107
Written Expression	90
Mathematics	105
Math Fluency	122

Beery-Buktenica Developmental Test of Visual-Motor Integration, Sixth Edition (VMI-VI)

	Standard Score
Beery Visual-Motor Integration Score	77

Peabody Picture Vocabulary Test, Fourth Edition

The PPVT-4 is a measure of receptive (hearing) vocabulary, which is used to assess one's verbal ability. The examinee is shown several different pictures of scenes or objects and is asked to point to the picture that represents the word given verbally.

Raw Score	Standard Score
185	102

Expressive Vocabulary Test, Second Edition

The EVT-2 measures expressive (spoken) vocabulary and word retrieval ability. The examinee is shown various scenes or objects and is asked to respond using a single word to questions about a label for a picture, what is going on in a scene, or provide a synonym for a word that fits the context of a scene.

Raw Score	Standard Score
142	104

Conners Continuous Performance Test-III

The Conners CPT-III is a computerized visual performance test that examines sustained attention and impulse control.

Measure	T-Score
Detectability	58
Omissions	52
Commissions	59
Perseverations	55
Hit Reaction Time	48
Hit Reaction Time Standard Deviation	57
Variability	62
Hit Reaction Time Block Change	52
Hit Reaction Time Interstimulus Interval Change	59

Conners Continuous Auditory Test of Attention

The Conners CATA is a computerized auditory performance test that assesses auditory processing and attention.

Measure	T-Score
Detectability	55
Omissions	44
Commissions	50
Perseverations	54
Hit Reaction Time	42
Hit Reaction Time Standard Deviation	56
Hit Reaction Time Block Change	58

Wisconsin Card Sorting Test

The WCST is used to assess executive functioning, the ability to shift and maintain problem-solving strategies for abstract problems when given feedback. A computerized 128-card version of the test was used for this evaluation.

Measure	Raw Score	T-Score
Total Categories Completed	6	
Number of Trials to Complete First Category	11	
Total Number Correct	88	
Total Percent Correct	83	
Total Number Errors	18	57
Total Percent Errors	17	59
Total of Perseverative Responses	8	60
Total of Perseverative Errors	8	59
Total Percent Perseverative Errors	8	60
Total Nonperseverative Error	10	53
Total of Other Responses	2	
Percent Conceptual Level Response	76	55
Total of Failure to Maintain Sets	2	
Learning to Learn Score	0	

Conners 3 Rating Scales

Parent Form

The Conners 3 Parent Rating Scale provides information about a child's behavior from a parent's point of view.

Scale	T-Score
Inattention	92
Hyperactivity or Impulsivity	103
Learning Problems	91
Executive Functioning	84
Aggression	68
Peer Relations	70
Global Index Total	96
DSM-IV Inattentive	89
DSM-IV Hyperactivity or Impulsivity	100
DSM-IV Conduct Disorder	50
DSM-IV Oppositional Defiant Disorder	77

Validity Scales	Raw Score	Cut-Off Score
Positive Impression	0	≥4
Negative Impression	2	≥3
Inconsistency Index	2	≥6
Symptom Counts		
Inattentive ADHD Symptoms	9	≥6
Hyperactive or Impulsive ADHD Symptoms	9	≥6
Conduct Disorder Symptoms	1	≥3
Oppositional Defiant Disorder Symptoms	7	≥4
Functional Impairment		
Schoolwork or Grades	3	3 = Sig. Impairment
Friendships or Relationships	3	3 = Sig. Impairment
Home Life	3	3 = Sig. Impairment
Conners ADHD Probability Percentage	99	

Teacher Form

The Conners 3 Teacher Rating Scale provides information about a child's behavior from a teacher's point of view. The form was completed by the client's reading, math, language therapy, and language arts teachers. Charlie's math and language arts teachers responded in a consistent and reliable fashion. Both of these teachers endorsed items indicating problems with attention indicating an inability to stay focused and on task during class. Additionally, these instructors indicated significant problems relating to his ability to learn and understand the material that is taught within the classroom. Furthermore, Charlie reportedly has trouble with controlling his anger and frustration directed toward his peers and teachers, especially his math and language arts instructors. Finally, both teachers indicated that he behaves in a manner that is consistent with those that exhibit oppositional and defiant behavior. T-scores of 70 and above are greater than expected. A complete list of scores is as follows.

Scale	Reading	Math	Language Arts
	T-Score	T-Score	T-Score
Inattention	72	77	69
Hyperactivity or Impulsivity	62	67	64

(*Continued*)

(Continued)

Learning Problems	89	89	92	
Executive Functioning	69	70	68	
Aggression	75	123	71	
Peer Relations	69	69	69	
Global Index Total	75	85	80	
DSM-IV Inattentive	63	81	76	
DSM-IV Hyperactivity or Impulsivity	68	70	70	
DSM-IV Conduct Disorder	71	56	50	
DSM-IV Oppositional Defiant Disorder	114	131	87	
Validity Scales	**Raw Score**	**Raw Score**	**Raw Score**	**Cut-Off Score**
Positive Impression	0	0	0	≥4
Negative Impression	2	5	2	≥3
Inconsistency Index	15	2	2	≥6
Symptom Counts				
Inattentive ADHD Symptoms	4	8	8	≥6
Hyperactive or Impulsive ADHD Symptoms	6	5	5	≥6
Conduct Disorder Symptoms	2	1	0	≥3
Oppositional Defiant Disorder Symptoms	5	7	6	≥4
Functional Impairment				
Schoolwork or Grades	2	3	2	3 = Sig. Impairment
Friendships or Relationships	2	1	1	3 = Sig. Impairment
Conners ADHD Probability Percentage	87	84	73	

Summary of Test Results

Neuropsychological testing revealed Charlie's overall level of intellectual functioning to be in the average range. He showed difficulties on timed visual spatial tasks, particularly when putting blocks together to replicate a picture, under timed conditions. He also showed weakness on his coding task, indicating he has difficulties with speeded graphomotor tasks.

However, when he only had to mark a line through the stimuli (Symbol Search) he did not show any limitations. His auditory memory fell in the high average range while his visual memory was in the average range, identifying a relative weakness for him. His ability to use recognition abilities after a delay was in the average range as were his attention and concentration.

An extensive test of Charlie's academic achievement in a variety of areas, including tests involving word identification, fluency and comprehension as well as mathematical calculations and fluency, and spelling and writing fluency (WIAT-III) showed that his reading and mathematics abilities were within expected levels. He had no difficulty with reading aloud, reading comprehension, speeded math, untimed math concepts, or spelling. For Charlie, his difficulty lies within his ability to express himself in a written format. His ability to compose an essay was severely below expected levels. Not only did he have difficulty composing his essay, he had poor penmanship and legibility was an issue. He evidenced difficulty with grammar and punctuation, often printing random letters in uppercase. On a measure of graphomotor processing, he performed in the below average range, and tasks of motor integration, such as writing, will result in a struggle for him. Measures of expressive and receptive language were within the average range. Scores on the CPT-III, measuring visual sustained attention, do not show any evidence of difficulties and neither did a measure of sustained auditory attention CATA. With regards to executive functioning, Charlie scored within the average range on all measures, and no deficits were exhibited.

Charlie's mother appears to have difficulty with coping when Charlie doesn't want to engage in academic tasks, especially writing, and her frustrations are evident on parent rating scales. She endorsed his significant attentional issues as well as inability to sit still, excessive fidgeting, and impulsiveness. In addition, she reported problems at school such as learning and understanding different concepts, completing homework and handing it in on time. She indicated problems with problem solving, inhibiting his behaviors, and making accurate judgments. She also stated that Charlie is often defiant and engages in annoying behaviors despite her efforts in trying to curb this conduct. Charlie's teachers also showed concerns on their rating scales; however, their responses were inconsistent and they evidenced a negative impression, likely reflecting their frustrations for his negative behavior when he is unable to complete work up to his own standards.

Diagnosis

Based on the results of the neuropsychological evaluation, a specific learning disorder, with impairment in written expression was considered. This disorder involves a level of writing as measured by standardized tests that is substantially below what is expected given the client's age, and causes significant difficulties with academics or activities of daily living. These difficulties must be evidenced on standardized achievement measures and clinical assessment. The learning difficulties typically begin during school age years but may not fully manifest until the child is faced with tasks such as timed tests, writing lengthy reports, or heavy academic loads. Impairment in written expression is generally a combination of difficulties in the individual's ability to compose written texts evidenced by grammatical or punctuation errors within sentences, poor paragraph organization, multiple spelling errors, and excessively poor handwriting. The individual's poor handwriting includes letters of the alphabet that are reversed, letters of the alphabet that are rotated, letters of the alphabet that are unrecognizable, and random mixture of cursive and printed letters.

Charlie's mother and teachers have always shown concern over his academic abilities, particularly with regard to his writing abilities. Charlie has also repeated the third grade due to failing state mandated testing. Charlie is currently on an IEP, which allows for additional time, oral responses, dictation of essay answers, frequent breaks, and small group settings.

Results from neuropsychological testing indicate that he has a deficit in his overall writing ability. Charlie exhibited intellectual abilities in the average range (FSIQ = 102) with no significant discrepancies. However, on academic testing, his writing difficulties are apparent. On the WIAT-III he exhibited difficulties in essay composition (SS = 76), including his ability to write an adequate number of words (SS = 71). While his theme development and ability to organize his thoughts were better, it was still lower than expected levels (SS = 86). He also showed difficulty with visual-motor integration (SS = 77) far below expected levels given his age. This is likely causing him some difficulty with his ability to quickly write essays. Based on these results and in conjunction with prior history of difficulty in areas of writing, Charlie meets the criteria of specific learning disorder, with impairment in written expression.

Specific Learning Disorder, with Impairment in Mathematics—Maggie, 8 Years Old

Maggie is an 8-year-old, right-handed, Caucasian female brought by her mother for an evaluation due to problems with math ability and inattention. Her mother stated that in kindergarten she began to have difficulties counting, doing simple addition, and recalling names of shapes. In first grade, it was suggested that Maggie repeat the grade due to her difficulties with numbers, but her mother did not feel it was necessary.

According to her school records, a Benchmark Individual Student Report was provided and her math scores fell within the 14th percentile while her reading scores fell within the 50th percentile. Overall, her math scores suggested that she was in danger of being retained once again and the school suggested a neuropsychological evaluation to help determine a need for accommodations.

Test Results

Stanford Binet Intelligence Scales, Fifth Edition

The Stanford Binet Intelligence Scales, Fifth Edition (SB-5) measures a person's general verbal and nonverbal intellectual abilities.

Nonverbal Index	Score	Verbal Index	Score
Fluid Reasoning	12	Fluid Reasoning	11
Knowledge	9	Knowledge	10
Quantitative Reasoning	8	Quantitative Reasoning	8
Visuospatial	9	Visuospatial	9
Working Memory	12	Working Memory	10

(*Continued*)

(Continued)

Index Scores	Score
Full Scale IQ	98
Nonverbal IQ	100
Verbal IQ	97
Fluid Reasoning	109
Knowledge	97
Quantitative Reasoning	89
Visuospatial	94
Working Memory	106

Wide Range Assessment of Memory and Learning, Second Edition

The WRAML-2 is used to assess memory function.

Core Subtests	Scaled Score	Recognition Subtests	Scaled Score
Story Memory	12	Story Recognition	7
Design Memory	10	Design Recognition	11
Verbal Learning	13	Verbal Learning Recognition	13
Picture Memory	9	Picture Memory Recognition	9
Finger Windows	12		
Number-Letter	8		
Delay Recall Subtests	**Scaled Score**		
Story Memory Recall	12		
Verbal Learning Recall	14		

Index Scores	Standard Score
General Memory	105
Verbal Memory	114
Visual Memory	97
Attention or Concentration	100
Verbal Recognition	99
Visual Recognition	100
General Recognition	99
Screening	114

Woodcock-Johnson Tests of Achievement, Third Edition

The Woodcock-Johnson Tests of Achievement, Third Edition is an extensive test of Maggie's academic achievement in a variety of areas, including tests involving word identification, fluency and comprehension as well as mathematical calculations and fluency, and spelling and writing fluency.

Clusters	Standard Score	Subtest	Standard Score
Broad Math	82	Letter-Word Identification	93
Broad Written Language	94	Reading Fluency	91
Broad Reading	92	Calculation	77
Math Calculation Skills	78	Math Fluency	82
Written Expression	92	Spelling Writing Fluency Passage Comprehension Applied Problems	92 101 96 80
		Writing Samples	99

Conners Continuous Auditory Test of Attention

The Conners CATA is a computerized auditory performance test that assesses auditory processing and attention.

Measure	T-Score
Detectability	55
Omissions	45
Commissions	47
Perseverations	59
Hit Reaction Time	34
Hit Reaction Time Standard Deviation	53
Hit Reaction Time Block Change	60

Conners Continuous Performance Test III

The Conners CPT-III is a computerized visual performance test that examines sustained attention and impulse control.

Measure	T-Score
Detectability	54
Omissions	44
Commissions	56
Perseverations	58
Hit Reaction Time	50
Hit Reaction Time Standard Deviation	47
Variability	44
Hit Reaction Time Block Change	45
Hit Reaction Time Interstimulus Interval Change	43
Level of Attention Deficits	None

Wisconsin Card Sorting Test

The WCST is used to assess executive functioning, namely the ability to shift and maintain problem-solving strategies for abstract problems when given feedback. A computerized 128-card version of the test was used for this evaluation.

Measure	Raw	T-Score
Total Categories Completed	6	-
Number of Trials to Complete First Category	14	
Total Number Correct	66	
Total Percent Correct	79	
Total Number Errors	18	61
Total Percent Errors	21	59
Total Number Perseverative Responses	10	58
Total Number Perseverative Errors	9	59
Total Percent Perseverative Errors	11	56
Total Number Nonperseverative Errors	9	59
Percent Conceptual Level Response	74	59
Total of Failure to Maintain Sets	0	
Learning to Learn Score	−2.71	N/A

Conners 3 Rating Scales

Parent Form

The Conners 3 Parent Rating Scale provides information about a child's behavior from a parent's point of view. Maggie's mother's test scores appear as follows.

Scale	T-Score	
Inattention	59	
Hyperactivity or Impulsivity	50	
Learning Problems	76	
Executive Functioning	52	
Aggression	46	
Peer Relations	60	
Global Index Total	40	
DSM-IV Inattentive	48	
DSM-IV Hyperactivity or Impulsivity	54	
DSM-IV Conduct Disorder	43	
DSM-IV Oppositional Defiant Disorder	45	
Validity Scales	**Raw Score**	**Cut-Off Score**
Positive Impression	1	≥4
Negative Impression	0	≥3
Inconsistency Index	3	≥6
Symptom Counts		
Inattentive ADHD Symptoms	1	≥6
Hyperactive or Impulsive ADHD Symptoms	2	≥6
Conduct Disorder Symptoms	0	≥3
Oppositional Defiant Disorder Symptoms	1	≥4
Functional Impairment		
Schoolwork or Grades	0	3 = Sig. Impairment
Friendships or Relationships	0	3 = Sig. Impairment
Home Life	0	3 = Sig. Impairment
Conners ADHD Probability Percentage	51	

Personality Inventory for Children, Second Edition

The PIC-2 is an objective measure used for child personality assessment.

Scale	T-Score	Scale	T-Score
INC (Inconsistency)	51	RLT (Reality Distortion)	45
FB (Dissimulation)	50	Rlt1 (Developmental Deviate)	47
DEF (Defensiveness)	54	Rlt2 (Hallucination or Delusion)	44
COG (Cognitive Impairment)	74	SOM (Somatic Concern)	44
Cog1 (Inadequate Abilities)	71	Som1 (Psychosomatic)	47
Cog2 (Poor Achievement)	77	Som2 (Muscle Tension or Anxiety)	42
Cog3 (Developmental Delay)	56	DIS (Psychological Discomfort)	53
ADH (Impulsivity or Distractible)	50	Dis1 (Fear or Worry)	61
Adh1 (Disruptive Behavior)	52	Dis2 (Depression)	46
Adh2 (Fearlessness)	42	Dis3 (Sleep or Death Concern)	54
DLQ (Delinquency)	44	WDL (Social Withdrawal)	56
Dlq1 (Antisocial)	46	Wdl1 (Social Introversion)	62
Dlq2 (Dyscontrol)	43	Wdl2 (Isolation)	41
Dlq3 (Noncompliance)	45	SSK (Social Skill Deficits)	60
FAM (Family Dysfunction)	47	Ssk1 (Limited Peer Status)	62
Fam1 (Member Conflicts)	50	Ssk2 (Conflict with Peers)	52
Fam2 (Parent Maladjustment)	43		

Summary of Test Results

Neuropsychological testing revealed Maggie's overall level of intellectual functioning to be in the average range. While there are no significant discrepancies between her abilities, she does show difficulties in verbal and nonverbal quantitative reasoning, which measures her ability to count, name numbers, and solve basic math problems. Her ability to recall information presented in an oral fashion was 1 standard deviation above her ability to recall information presented in a visual manner, which may shine some light on to why recalling math concepts is difficult for her.

Math is taught in a very visual manner, especially in early school years when children are learning to add and subtract and lining up numbers in simple math equations. She did not evidence any significant difficulties with immediate recall or delayed recognition.

On a measure of academic achievement in a variety of areas, including tests involving word identification, fluency and comprehension as well as mathematical calculations and fluency, and spelling and writing fluency (WCJ-III-ACH), Maggie exhibited average abilities in areas of reading, writing, and spelling, consistent with expected levels given her age. However, she exhibited difficulties in both timed and untimed measures of mathematical abilities. She evidenced difficulty performing foundational mathematical computations and speeded addition, subtraction, and multiplication facts. She showed a weakness in comprehending the nature of the problem, sorting out relevant information, and stating the solution. Scores on the CPT-III, measuring visual sustained attention, do not show any evidence of difficulties and neither did a measure of sustained auditory attention (CATA). With regards to executive functioning, Maggie scored within the average range on all measures and no deficits were exhibited.

Maggie's mother completed parent rating forms and only showed concern over her daughter's poor academic achievement and learning abilities. This is consistent with verbal teacher reports who noted that overall Maggie is a great student who likes to learn, but has difficulty with grasping mathematical concepts.

Diagnosis

Based on the reported history and records provided, a diagnosis of specific learning disorder, with impairment in mathematics, was considered. This disorder involves difficulty learning and using academic skills, which have persisted for a six-month period, despite the provision of interventions that target the specific difficulties. This disturbance also is substantially below the expected level given the client's chronological age, and causes significant interference with academic or occupational performance or with activities of daily living, as confirmed by individually administered standardized achievement measures and clinical assessment. Signs associated with a specific learning disorder, with impairment in mathematics, include difficulty with number sense, math reasoning, fluent calculation, or memorization of arithmetic facts.

Results of the neuropsychological evaluation suggest that Maggie has difficulties in both timed and untimed mathematics. When compared to her overall FSIQ score of 98 on the SB-5, her calculation (SS = 77), math fluency (SS = 82), and applied problems (SS = 80) abilities as measured by the Woodcock-Johnson Achievement (WCJ-ACH) are well below expected levels, given her intellectual ability and expected performance based on her age. She appears to have deficits in the fundamental, foundational aspects of mathematics as she is evidencing difficulties on some of the earliest portions of the subtests. Based on these results, Maggie meets criteria for a specific learning disorder, with impairment in mathematics.

High Intelligence with Specific Learning Disorder—Martin, 15 Years Old

Martin is a 15-year-old, right-handed, Hispanic male brought in by his parents for an evaluation to update testing on his current academic functioning to determine if he qualifies for accommodations. According to Martin's parents, he was born premature at 34 weeks due to cholestasis of pregnancy. Martin remained in the intensive care unit for 10 days due to amniotic fluid in his lungs, which was treated with antibiotics.

At the age of 6, Martin was referred for an evaluation by his guidance counselor. According to his parents, he was not functioning up to his potential and exhibited difficulty controlling and keeping his hands to himself with his peers, was restless and fidgety when seated, and had difficulty listening. In addition, he often did what he wanted rather than what he was asked to do, displayed carelessness, was inconsistent in his performance and his ability to concentrate and control his behavior, avoided tasks that he was not interested in, was easily distractible, had difficulty staying on task, was messy and disorganized, often lost, forgot, or misplaced things, and had difficulty delaying his emotional expression. Following his evaluation, he was diagnosed with Attention-Deficit/

Hyperactivity Disorder, Combined Type and was prescribed Adderall to manage his behavioral symptoms at the age of 8 years. When Martin was 11, his parents began to feel as though the medication was not effective. After seeking consultation with a psychiatrist, Martin began taking Concerta (36 mg), which he has been on since.

Martin reported that he has a difficult time organizing his thoughts to start his work or tests. He stated that as a result, it takes a lot of time to begin and that he often runs out of time, which results in his being unable to check over or finish his work. He further noted that he has a difficult time getting to and staying focused on his homework, as he is easily distracted. He noted that recently his math teacher gave him extra time and he was able to get all of the answers correct.

Test Results

Wechsler Intelligence Scale for Children, Fourth Edition

The WISC-IV is a measure of general intellectual functioning. With a chronological age of 15 years, Martin's overall level of functioning was in the very superior range. Complete scores are listed as follows.

Verbal Comprehension Subtests	Score	Perceptual Reasoning Subtests	Score
Vocabulary	14	Block Design	11
Similarities	17	Picture Concepts	15
Comprehension	17	Matrices	18
Working Memory Subtests	**Score**	**Processing Speed Subtests**	**Score**
Digit Span	14	Digit Symbol Coding	11
Letter or Number Sequencing	14	Symbol Search	13
Index Scores		**Score**	
Full Scale IQ		132	
Verbal Comprehension		136	
Perceptual Reasoning		129	
Working Memory		123	
Processing Speed		106	

Wide Range Assessment of Memory and Learning, Second Edition

The WRAML-2 is used to assess memory function. Martin performed in the very superior range of functioning with regards to his overall memory. Complete scores are listed as follows.

Core Subtests	Scaled Score	Recognition Subtests	Scaled Score
Story Memory	15	Story Recognition	13
Design Memory	11	Design Recognition	10
Verbal Learning	15	Verbal Learning Recognition	13
Picture Memory	13	Picture Memory Recognition	10
Finger Windows	17		
Number-Letter	17		
Delay Recall Subtests	**Scaled Score**		
Story Memory Recall	13		
Verbal Learning Recall	14		

Index Scores	Standard Score
General Memory	135
Verbal Memory	129
Visual Memory	112
Attention or Concentration	138
Verbal Recognition	118
Visual Recognition	100
General Recognition	111
Screening	125

Woodcock-Johnson Cognitive, Third Edition

The WJC-III is a test that assesses many aspects of cognitive functioning including visual spatial thinking, auditory processing, fluid reasoning, and processing speed. Martin's overall level of cognitive functioning fell in the superior range. Complete test scores are listed as follows.

Clusters	Standard Score	Subtest	Standard Score
General Intellectual Ability	127	Verbal Comprehension	111
Verbal Ability	111	Visual-Auditory Learn	114
Thinking Ability	131	Spatial Relations	130
Cognitive Efficiency	124	Sound Blending	127
Phonemic Awareness	131	Concept Formation	115
Working Memory	135	Visual Matching	101
		Numbers Reversed	132
		Incomplete Words	118
		Aud. Work Memory	127

Woodcock-Johnson Tests of Achievement, Third Edition

The Woodcock-Johnson Tests of Achievement, Third Edition is an extensive test of a client's academic achievement in a variety of areas, including tests involving word identification, fluency, and comprehension as well as mathematical calculations and fluency, and spelling and writing fluency. Martin performed in the above average range in overall academic abilities. Complete scores are listed as follows.

Clusters	Standard Score	Subtest	Standard Score
Total Achievement	120	Letter-Word Identification	112
Oral Language	128	Reading Fluency	94
Broad Math	128	Story Recall	104
Broad Written Language	112	Understanding Directions	133
Broad Reading	105	Calculation	132
		Math Fluency	92
		Spelling	120
		Writing Fluency	102
		Passage Comprehension	120
		Applied Problems	131
		Writing Samples	108

Nelson Denny Reading Test

The NDRT is an assessment of an individual's ability in three areas of academic achievement: vocabulary, reading comprehension, and reading rate.

Standard Administration			
Test	Raw	Standard Score	Grade Equivalent
Vocabulary	50	111	13.3
Comprehension	30	92	8.3
Reading Rate	106	77	-
Total	80	101	10.4

Extended Administration			
Test	Raw	Standard Score	Grade Equivalent
Vocabulary	69	131	17.1
Comprehension	54	112	14.1
Total	123	121	15.6

Conners Continuous Performance Test II

The Conners Continuous Performance Test II is a computer-based test of visual attention.

Measure	T-Score	Measure	T-Score
Omission Percentage	45	Perseveration Percentage	46
Commissions Percentage	33	Hit Response Time Block Change	48
Hit Reaction Time	56	Hit Standard Error Block Change	46
Hit Reaction Time Standard Error	42	Hit Response Time Inter-stimulus Interval Change	54
Variability	34	Hit Standard Error Inter-stimulus Interval Change	45
Detectability	31	ADHD Score	50
Response Style	40	Neurological Score	-

Wisconsin Card Sorting Test

The WCST is used to assess executive functioning, the ability to shift and maintain problem-solving strategies for abstract problems when given feedback. A computerized 128-card version of the test was used for this evaluation.

Measure	Raw Score	Standard Score
Total Categories Completed	6	
Number of Trials to Complete 1st Category	70	
Total Number Correct	62	
Total Percent Correct	89	
Total Number Errors	8	67
Total Percent Errors	11	68
Total of Perseverative Responses	5	68
Total of Perseverative Errors	5	68
Total Percent Perseverative Errors	7	63
Total Nonperseverative Error	3	65
Total of Other Responses	0	
Percent Conceptual Level Response	87	66
Total of Failure to Maintain Sets	0	
Learning to Learn Score	0	

Conners 3 Rating Scales

Parent Form

The Conners 3 Parent Rating Scale provides information about a child's behavior from a parent's point of view.

The client's mother's test scores appear as follows.

Scale	T-Score
Inattention	81
Hyperactivity or Impulsivity	56
Learning Problems	65

(*Continued*)

(Continued)

Executive Functioning	72	
Aggression	45	
Peer Relations	75	
Global Index Total	63	
DSM-IV Inattentive	78	
DSM-IV Hyperactivity or Impulsivity	57	
DSM-IV Conduct Disorder	43	
DSM-IV Oppositional Defiant Disorder	47	
Validity Scales	**Raw Score**	**Cut-Off Score**
Positive Impression	0	≥ 4
Negative Impression	1	≥ 3
Inconsistency Index	5	≥ 6
Symptom Counts		
Inattentive ADHD Symptoms	6	≥ 6
Hyperactive or Impulsive ADHD Symptoms	2	≥ 6
Conduct Disorder Symptoms	0	≥ 3
Oppositional Defiant Disorder Symptoms	0	≥ 4
Functional Impairment		
Schoolwork or Grades	1	3 = Sig. Impairment
Friendships or Relationships	1	3 = Sig. Impairment
Home Life	1	3 = Sig. Impairment
Conners ADHD Probability Percentage	56	

The client's father's scores are as follows.

Scale	T-Score
Inattention	71
Hyperactivity or Impulsivity	58
Learning Problems	53
Executive Functioning	74
Aggression	43
Peer Relations	75
Global Index Total	63
DSM-IV Inattentive	78
DSM-IV Hyperactivity or Impulsivity	60

DSM-IV Conduct Disorder	43	
DSM-IV Oppositional Defiant Disorder	47	
Validity Scales	**Raw Score**	**Cut-Off Score**
Positive Impression	1	≥4
Negative Impression	0	≥3
Inconsistency Index	7	≥6
Symptom Counts		
Inattentive ADHD Symptoms	6	≥6
Hyperactive or Impulsive ADHD Symptoms	2	≥6
Conduct Disorder Symptoms	0	≥3
Oppositional Defiant Disorder Symptoms	0	≥4
Functional Impairment		
Schoolwork or Grades	2	3 = Sig. Impairment
Friendships or Relationships	2	3 = Sig. Impairment
Home Life	0	3 = Sig. Impairment
Conners ADHD Probability Percentage	51	

Teacher Form

The Conners 3 Teacher Rating Scale provides information about a child's behavior from a teacher's point of view.

The client's math teacher's test scores are as follows.

Scale	T-Score
Inattention	57
Hyperactivity or Impulsivity	49
Learning Problems	51
Executive Functioning	60
Aggression	46
Peer Relations	49
Global Index Total	48
DSM-IV Inattentive	60
DSM-IV Hyperactivity or Impulsivity	51
DSM-IV Conduct Disorder	45
DSM-IV Oppositional Defiant Disorder	45

(Continued)

(Continued)

Validity Scales	Raw Score	Cut-Off Score
Positive Impression	1	≥4
Negative Impression	0	≥3
Inconsistency Index	4	≥6
Symptom Counts		
Inattentive ADHD Symptoms	1	≥6
Hyperactive or Impulsive ADHD Symptoms	1	≥6
Conduct Disorder Symptoms	0	≥3
Oppositional Defiant Disorder Symptoms	0	≥4
Functional Impairment		
Schoolwork or Grades	0	3 = Sig. Impairment
Friendships or Relationships	0	3 = Sig. Impairment
Conners ADHD Probability Percentage	51	

The client's writing and rhetoric teacher's test scores are as follows.

Scale	T-Score
Inattention	57
Hyperactivity or Impulsivity	55
Learning Problems	63
Executive Functioning	56
Aggression	53
Peer Relations	70
Global Index Total	54
DSM-IV Inattentive	55
DSM-IV Hyperactivity or Impulsivity	58
DSM-IV Conduct Disorder	57
DSM-IV Oppositional Defiant Disorder	51

Validity Scales	Raw Score	Cut-Off Score
Positive Impression	0	≥4
Negative Impression	2	≥3
Inconsistency Index	5	≥6
Symptom Counts		
Inattentive ADHD Symptoms	0	≥6
Hyperactive or Impulsive ADHD Symptoms	1	≥6

Conduct Disorder Symptoms	-	≥3
Oppositional Defiant Disorder Symptoms	0	≥4
Functional Impairment		
Schoolwork or Grades	1	3 = Sig. Impairment
Friendships or Relationships	1	3 = Sig. Impairment
Conners ADHD Probability Percentage	19	

The client's physics teacher's test scores are as follows.

Scale	T-Score	
Inattention	57	
Hyperactivity or Impulsivity	54	
Learning Problems	51	
Executive Functioning	51	
Aggression	49	
Peer Relations	60	
Global Index Total	54	
DSM-IV Inattentive	57	
DSM-IV Hyperactivity or Impulsivity	51	
DSM-IV Conduct Disorder	45	
DSM-IV Oppositional Defiant Disorder	45	
Validity Scales	**Raw Score**	**Cut-Off Score**
Positive Impression	0	≥4
Negative Impression	0	≥3
Inconsistency Index	4	≥6
Symptom Counts		
Inattentive ADHD Symptoms	1	≥6
Hyperactive or Impulsive ADHD Symptoms	1	≥6
Conduct Disorder Symptoms	0	≥3
Oppositional Defiant Disorder Symptoms	0	≥4
Functional Impairment		
Schoolwork or Grades	2	3 = Sig. Impairment
Friendships or Relationships	1	3 = Sig. Impairment
Conners ADHD Probability Percentage	39	

Minnesota Multiphasic Personality Inventory-Adolescent

The Minnesota Multiphasic Personality Inventory-Adolescent (MMPI-A) is an assessment that elicits a wide range of self-descriptions scored to give a quantitative measurement of an individual's level of emotional adjustment and attitude toward test taking.

Scale	T-Score	Scale	T-Score
L (Lie)	55	4 (Psychopathic Deviate)	33
F (Infrequency)	40	5 (Masculinity or Femininity)	54
K (Correction)	68	6 (Paranoia)	46
VRIN	45	7 (Psychasthenia)	42
TRIN	51	8 (Schizophrenia)	40
1 (Hypochondriasis)	43	9 (Hypomania)	46
2 (Depression)	43	0 (Social Introversion)	49
3 (Hysteria)	45		

Test of Memory Malingering

The TOMM is used to assess the degree of effort displayed by a client on memory tasks. Martin scored in the normal range on this test. Trial 2 or retention scores below 45 are considered questionable. Complete scores are listed as follows.

Trial	Score
Trial 1	50
Trial 2	50
Retention Trial	50

Summary of Test Results

Testing revealed that Martin has a FSIQ in the very superior range with consistent abilities across all domains. An additional measure of cognitive functioning (Woodcock Johnson Cognitive, WCJ-COG) showed commensurate abilities, with a general intellectual ability score in the Superior range of functioning. On a measure of memory function, Martin also scored in the superior range when asked to recall information that was presented to him in a verbal manner and in the high average range when asked to recall information presented in a visual manner. He did not display any difficulties with his attention or concentration as those scores fell in the very superior range.

When given an extensive measure of academic abilities in a variety of areas (WCJ-Ach), Martin exhibited difficulties almost across the board. On math portions of the measure, he performed in the superior range when answering complex mathematical facts and equations and was able to comprehend the nature of a math problem, identify relevant information, and state the solutions. However, he spent a painstakingly amount of time on each question and solved problems by working backwards, counting on his fingers, or adding instead of multiplying. When faced with a timed math measure, he performed in the average range, far below expected levels. Writing samples proved to be a challenge for Martin. He displayed difficulty when asked to quickly write simple sentences and when asked to produce written sentences in response to prompts that increased in difficulty. With regards to reading, Martin exhibited above average decoding skills and was able to adequately read a short passage and supply a key missing word when he was not under time constraints. However, reading speed and automaticity fell in the average range. On a second measure of speeded reading (NDRT), for the standard time administration (15-minute vocabulary, 20-minute comprehension), his overall performance was in the average range. He performed in the high average range when asked to identify definitions for words. He performed in the average range when asked to answer questions about narrative passages. In addition, he had a below average reading rate. When provided with 60 percent extra time on the extended administration (24-minute vocabulary, 32-minute comprehension), his scores significantly increased. He performed in the superior range when identifying definitions for words and in the high average range when answering questions about complex narrative passages. On measures of attention and executive functioning, Martin did not exhibit any difficulties.

On parent report forms (Conners 3), his mother indicated poor concentration, difficulties with peers, difficulty finishing projects, and poor planning abilities. His father responded in an inconsistent manner. Several of Martin's teachers also completed the behavior scale and indicated poor social skills and difficulty with peer relations. On an objective personality measure, Martin responded in a defensive manner and no clinically significant areas of concern were noted.

Diagnosis

Based on the reported history and test results, diagnoses of specific learning disorder, with impairment in reading, written expression, and mathematics were considered. Martin is a very bright child, with intelligence in the very superior range of functioning, but he is experiencing difficulties in school because he is unable to complete his work in a timely manner. With regards to reading, he exhibits a slow reading rate and fluency and is able to demonstrate his abilities when provided with extra time, as seen on the NDRT. When completing math tasks, he has difficulties with the foundational skills to correctly answer math problems in a quick and useful manner, appearing as though he never learned the correct way to solve basic math problems. On measures of written expression, he exhibited difficulty with grammar, sentence composition, and clarity of thoughts.

Martin falls into a class of children with learning disabilities that has recently begun to garner a lot of attention. Martin, even with his difficulties under time constraints, falls in the average range for reading, math, and writing abilities, and some would say he should not receive extra time or accommodations because he is performing at a level expected for his age. However, this is a disservice to Martin as he can clearly perform at a level consistent with his intellectual abilities when he is provided extra time, and he should be given the chance to achieve at his full potential, like any other child who has been diagnosed with a learning disability. His weaknesses become especially apparent and disheartening for him in an academic setting in which he is graded on his performance and most importantly has his performance compared to that of others. He currently attends a stressful and challenging high school in which a majority of the students are of similar intellectual levels as him. Thus, there is a great deal of competition and pressure to be a high achieving student; being a slow reader, underachieving in academic areas as opposed to honors classes, negatively affected him.

References

AERA, APA, and NCME (American Educational Research Association, American Psychological Association, National Council on Measurement in Education), Joint Committee on Standards for Educational, and Psychological Testing (US). 1999. Standards for Educational and Psychological Testing. American Educational Research Association.

Altarac, M., and E. Saroha. 2007. "Lifetime Prevalence of Learning Disability Among U.S. Children." *Pediatrics* 119, Supplement 1, pp. S77–83.

APA (American Psychiatric Association). 2000. *Diagnostic and Statistical Manual of Mental Disorders.* 4th ed., text rev. American Psychiatric Pub.

APA (American Psychiatric Association). 2013. *Diagnostic and Statistical Manual of Mental Disorders (DSM-5).* American Psychiatric Pub.

American Speech-Language-Hearing Association. 2016. *Spoken Language Disorders.* (Practice Portal). Retrieved January 12, 2016 from www.Practice-Portal/Clinical-Topics/Spoken-Language Disorders

Badian, N.A. 1983. "Dyscalculia and Nonverbal Disorders of Learning." *Progress in Learning Disabilities* 5, pp. 235–64.

Bauer, Daniel J., and Heathe Luz McNaughton Reyes. 2010. "Modeling Variability in Individual Development: Differences of Degree or Kind?" *Child Development Perspectives* 4, no. 2, pp. 114–22.

Beech, M. 2010. *Accommodations: Assisting Students with Disabilities.* Tallahassee, FL: Florida Department of Education.

Beech, M., D. Sue, and M. Jan. 2013. "Selecting Accommodations: Guidance for Individual Educational Plan Teams." Retrieved January 12, 2016 from www.fldoe.org/core/fileparse.php/7690/urlt/0070064-selectingaccommodations.pdf

Bolt, S. 2004. "Accommodations for Testing Students with Disabilities: Information For Parents." In *Helping Children at Home and School II: Handout for Families and Educators* (Spanish and English Edition) Ring-bound, eds. A. Canter, L. Paige, M. Roth, I. Romero, and S. Carroll. Bethesda, MD: National Association of School Psychologists.

Bracken, B.A., and R.S. McCallum. 1998. *Universal Nonverbal Intelligence Test.* Houghton-Mifflin.

Braden, J.P. 1994. *Deafness, Deprivation, and IQ.* Springer Science and Business Media.

Brown, J.I., V.V. Fishco, and G.S. Hanna. 1993. *Nelson-Denny Reading Test: Manual for Scoring and Interpretation, Forms G & H*. Riverside Publishing Company.

Brown, L., R.J. Sherbenou, and S.K. Johnsen. 2010. *TONI-4: Test of Nonverbal Intelligence*. Fourth Edition. Pro-E.

Connolly, A.J. 2007. *KeyMath 3: Diagnostic Assessment*. Bloomington, MN: Pearson.

Cortiella, C., and S.H. Horowitz. 2014. *The State of Learning Disabilities: Facts, Trends and Emerging Issues*. New York: National Center for Learning Disabilities.

de Filippo, C.L. 1982. "Memory for Articulated Sequences and Lipreading Performance of Hearing-Impaired Observers." *The Volta Review* 84, no. 3, pp. 134–46.

Devine, A., F. Soltész, A. Nobes, U. Goswami, and D. Szűcs. 2013. "Gender Differences in Developmental Dyscalculia Depend on Diagnostic Criteria." *Learning and Instruction* 27, pp. 31–39.

Dhanalakshmi, D. 2015. "Nonverbal Learning Disabilities." *Indian Journal of Health and Wellbeing* 6, no. 1, p. 109.

Dial, J.G., F. Chan, C. Mezger, and H.J. Parker. 1991. "Comprehensive Vocational Evaluation System for Visually Impaired and Blind Persons." *Journal of Visual Impairment and Blindness*.

Dowler, R.N., D.L. Harrington, K.Y. Haaland, R.M. Swanda, F. Fee, and K. Fiedler. 1997. "Profiles of Cognitive Functioning in Chronic Spinal Cord Injury and the Role of Moderating Variables." *Journal of the International Neuropsychological Society* 3, no. 5, pp. 464–72.

Drummond, C.R., S.A. Ahmad, and B.P. Rourke. 2005. "Rules for the Classification of Younger Children with Nonverbal Learning Disabilities and Basic Phonological Processing Disabilities." *Archives of Clinical Neuropsychology* 20, no. 2, pp. 171–82.

Dunn, D.M., and L.M. Dunn. 2007. *Peabody Picture Vocabulary Test: Manual*. Pearson.

Flanagan, D.P., and K.S. McGrew. 1997. "A Cross-Battery Approach to Assessing and Interpreting Cognitive Abilities: Narrowing the Gap Between Practice and Cognitive Science." In *Contemporary Intellectual Assessment: Theories, Tests, and Issues*, 314–25. New York: Guilford Press.

Fletcher, J.M., B.R. Foorman, A. Boudousquie, M.A. Barnes, C. Schatschneider, and D.J. Francis. 2002. "Assessment of Reading and Learning Disabilities a Research-Based Intervention-Oriented Approach." *Journal of School Psychology* 40, no. 1, pp. 27–63.

Florida Department of Education. 2013. *Portal to Exceptional Education Resources* [Computer software]. Tallahassee, FL: Author.

Friedlander, B. 2004. "Assistive Computer Technology: Introduction for Parents and Educators." In *Helping Children at Home and School II: Handout for Families and Educators* (Spanish and English Edition) Ring-bound, eds. A. Canter, L. Paige, M. Roth, I. Romero, and S. Carroll. Bethesda, MD: National Association of School Psychologists.

Geisinger, K.F., K. Kriegsman, G. Taliaferro, I.Z. Schultz, R.H. Hamilton, T. Heller, R. Hughes, and others authors. 2011. "Guidelines for Assessment of and Intervention with Persons with Disabilities." In *Assessing Students' Needs for Assistive Technology (ASNAT)*, ed. J. Gierach, June 2009. 5th ed. Retrieved from www.wati.org/content/supports/free/pdf/ASNAT5thEditionJun09.pdf

Gerlach, A.T., C.V. Murphy, and J.F. Dasta. 2009. "An Updated Focused Review of Dexmedetomidine in Adults." *Annals of Pharmacotherapy* 43, no. 12, pp. 2064–74.

Goldman, A.I., E. Margolis, R. Samuels, and S. Stich. 2012. "Theory of Mind." *The Oxford Handbook of Philosophy of Cognitive Science*, pp. 402–24.

Gross-Tsur, V., O. Manor, and R.S. Shalev. 1996. "Developmental Dyscalculia: Prevalence and Demographic Features." *Developmental Medicine & Child Neurology* 38, no. 1, pp. 25–33.

Hale, J.B., A. Kaufman, J.A. Naglieri, and K.A. Kavale. 2006. "Implementation of IDEA: Integrating Response to Intervention and Cognitive Assessment Methods." *Psychology in the Schools* 43, no. 7, pp. 753–70.

Hällgren, M., B. Larsby, B. Lyxell, and S. Arlinger. 2001. "Evaluation of a Cognitive Test Battery in Young and Elderly Normal-Hearing and Hearing-Impaired Persons." *Journal of the American Academy of Audiology* 12, no. 7, pp. 357–70.

Hammill, D.D., J. Lee Wiederholt, and E.A. Allen. 2006. "Test of Silent Word Reading Fluency." Austin, TX: Pro-Ed.

Handler, S.M., and W.M. Fierson. 2011. "Learning Disabilities, Dyslexia, and Vision." *Pediatrics* 127, no. 3, pp. e818–56.

Hein, J., M.W. Bzufka, and K.J. Neumärker. 2000. "The Specific Disorder of Arithmetic Skills. Prevalence Studies in a Rural and an Urban Population Sample and Their Clinico-Neuropsychological Validation." *European Child and Adolescent Psychiatry* 9, no. 2, pp. S87–101.

Hill-Briggs, F., J.G. Dial, D.A. Morere, and A. Joyce. 2007. "Neuropsychological Assessment of Persons with Physical Disability, Visual Impairment or Blindness, and Hearing Impairment or Deafness." *Archives of clinical neuropsychology* 22, no. 3, pp. 389–404.

Huntington, D.D., and W.N. Bender. 1993. "Adolescents with Learning Disabilities at Risk Emotional Well-Being, Depression, Suicide." *Journal of Learning Disabilities* 26, no. 3, pp. 159–66.

Individuals with Disabilities Education Act 2004. 20 U.S.C. § 1400.

Katusic, S.K., R.C. Colligan, A.L. Weaver, and W.J. Barbaresi. 2009. "The Forgotten Learning Disability: Epidemiology of Written-Language Disorder in a Population-Based Birth Cohort (1976–1982), Rochester, Minnesota." *Pediatrics* 123, no. 5, pp. 1306–13.

Kaufman, A.S. 2008. "Neuropsychology and Specific Learning Disabilities: Lessons from the Past as a Guide to Present Controversies and Future Clinical Practice." In *Neuropsychological Perspectives on Learning Disabilities in an Era of RTI: Recommendations for Diagnosis and Intervention,* eds. by E. Fletcher-Janzen and C. Reynolds, 1–13. Hoboken, NJ: Wiley.

Klin, A., F.R. Volkmar, and S.S. Sparrow, eds. 2000. *Asperger Syndrome.* New York: Guilford Press.

Kovas, Y., and R. Plomin. 2007. "Learning Abilities and Disabilities Generalist Genes, Specialist Environments." *Current Directions in Psychological Science* 16, no. 5, pp. 284–88.

Kupper, L. 2000. "A Guide to the Individualized Education Program." Retrieved July 7, 2016 from http://files.eric.ed.gov/fulltext/ED444279.pdf

Lazarus, S.S., M.L. Thurlow, K.E. Lail, K.D. Eisenbraun, and K. Kato. 2005. State policies on assessment participation and accommodations for students with disabilities (NCEO Synthesis Report 64). Minneapolis, MN: University of Minnesota, National Center on Educational Outcomes.

Lewis, C., G.J. Hitch, and P. Walker. 1994. "The Prevalence of Specific Arithmetic Difficulties and Specific Reading Difficulties in 9- to 10-Year-Old Boys and Girls." *Journal of Child Psychology and Psychiatry* 35, no. 2, pp. 283–92.

Lezak, M. 2004. *Neuropsychological Assessment.* New York: Oxford University Press.

Lukomski, J. 2004. "Hearing Loss: A Primer for Parents and Educators." In *Helping Children at Home and School II: Handout for Families and Educators* (Spanish and English Edition) Ring-bound, eds. A. Canter, L. Paige, M. Roth, I. Romero, and S. Carroll. Bethesda, MD: National Association of School Psychologists.

Martin F.J. 2004. "Developmental Dyslexia (specific reading difficulty)." In *Pediatric Ophthalmology and Strabismus,* eds. D. Taylor, and C. Hoyt. 3rd ed., 714–72. St Louis, MO: Saunders, Ltd.

Mather, N., D.D. Hammill, E.A. Allen, and R. Roberts. 2004. "TOSWRF: Test of silent word reading fluency: Examiner's manual." Austin, TX: Pro-Ed.

Miller, C.A., and G. Erin. 2008. "Comparison of Performance on Two Nonverbal Intelligence Tests by Adolescents with and Without Language Impairment." *Journal of Communication Disorders* 41, no. 4, pp. 358–71.

Moll, K., S. Kunze, N. Neuhoff, J. Bruder, and G. Schulte-Körne. 2014. "Specific Learning Disorder: Prevalence and Gender Differences." *PLoS one* 9, no. 7, e103537.

Morgan, S.K., and S. Klar. 2004. "Visual Impairments: Information for Parents and Teachers." In *Helping Children at Home and School II: Handout for Families and Educators* (Spanish and English Edition) Ring-bound, eds. A. Canter, L. Paige, M. Roth, I. Romero, and S. Carroll. Bethesda, MD: National Association of School Psychologists.

Nelson, M.J., J.I. Brown, and M.J. Denny. 1960. *The Nelson-Denny Reading Test: Vocabulary, Comprehension, Rate.* Oxfrod, England: Houghton Mifflin.

Newhall, P. 2013. "Language-Based Learning Disabilities and Academic Proficiency." Retrieved January 12, 2016 from www.iecaonline.com/blog/2013/04/01/language-based-learning-disabilities-and-academic-proficiency/

Ozonoff, S., and E.M. Griffith. 2000. "Neuropsychological Function and the External Validity of Asperger Syndrome." *Asperger Syndrome* pp. 72–96.

Patino, E. 2014. "Understanding Nonverbal Learning Disabilities." Retrieved January 12, 2016 from www.understood.org/en/learning-attention-issues/child-learning-disabilities/nonverbal-learning-disabilities/understanding-nonverbal-learning-disabilities

Pennington, B.F. 2006. "From Single to Multiple Deficit Models of Developmental Disorders." *Cognition* 101, no. 2, pp. 385–413.

Quinn, J.M., and R.K. Wagner. 2013. "Gender Differences in Reading Impairment and in the Identification of Impaired Readers: Results from a Large-Scale Study of at-Risk Readers." *Journal of learning disabilities* 0022219413508323.

Ramaa, S., and I. Gowramma. 2002. "A Systematic Procedure for Identifying and Classifying Children with Dyscalculia Among Primary School Children in India." *Dyslexia* 8, no. 2, pp. 67–85.

Reasonable Accommodations for Students with Disabilities. 2007. Retrieved January 12, 2016 http://www.spcollege.edu/central/hr/accommodations_manual.htm

Reitan, R., and L.A. Davison, eds. 1974. *Clinical Neuro-Psychology: Current Status and Applications.* WA DC: Winston.

Reynolds, C.R., and S.E. Shaywitz. 2009. "Response to Intervention: Ready or Not? Or, from Wait-to-Fail to Watch-Them-Fail." *School Psychology Quarterly* 24, no. 2, p. 130.

Roid, G.H., L.J. Miller, M. Pomplun, and C. Koch. 2013. *Leiter-3: Leiter International Performance Scale.* 3rd ed. Stoelting, Co.

Roman, M.A. 1998. "The Syndrome of Nonverbal Learning Disabilities: Clinical Description and Applied Aspects." *Current Issues in Education* 1, no. 7, pp. 1–20.

Rourke, B.P., ed. 1995. *Syndrome of Nonverbal Learning Disabilities: Neurodevelopmental Manifestations.* New York: Guilford Press.

Rourke, B.P. 2005. "Neuropsychology of Learning Disabilities: Past and Future." *Learning Disability Quarterly* 28, no. 2, pp. 111–14.

Rourke, B.P., and K.D. Tsatsanis. 1996. "Syndrome of Nonverbal Learning Disabilities: Psycholinguistic Assets and Deficits." *Topics in Language Disorders* 16, no. 2, pp. 30–44.

Rourke, B.P., and K.D. Tsatsanis. 2000. "Nonverbal Learning Disabilities and Asperger Syndrome." *Asperger Syndrome,* pp. 231–53.

Schneider, W.J., and K.S. McGrew. 2012. "The Cattell-Horn-Carroll Model of Intelligence." *Contemporary Intellectual Assessment: Theories, Tests, and,* 99–144. 3rd ed.

Schrank, F.A., N. Mather, and K.S. McGrew. 2014. *Woodcock-Johnson IV Tests of Achievement.* Rolling Meadows, IL: Riverside.

Schrank, F.A., N. Mather, and K.S. McGrew. 2014. *Woodcock-Johnson IV Tests of Cognitive Ability.* Rolling Meadows, IL: Riverside.

Shalev, R.S. 2004. "Developmental Dyscalculia." *Journal of Child Neurology* 19, no. 10, pp. 765–71.

Shapiro, B.K. 2004. "Cerebral Palsy: A Reconceptualization of the Spectrum." *The Journal of Pediatrics* 145, no. 2, pp. S3–7.

Spina Bifida Family Support. January 19, 2006. "Nonverbal Learning Disorder Syndrome." www.spinabifidasupport.com/nvldsyndrome.htm

St. Petersberg College. "Reasonable Accommodations for Students with Disabilities." Last modified September 2007 www.spcollege.edu/central/hr/accommodationsmanual.htm#motor

Swisher, L., E. Plante, and S. Lowell. 1994. "Nonlinguistic Deficits of Children With Language Disorders Complicate the Interpretation of Their Nonverbal IQ scores." *Language, Speech, and Hearing Services in Schools* 25, no. 4, pp. 235–40.

Tannock, R. 2014. "DSM-5 Changes in Diagnostic Criteria for Specific Learning Disabilities (SLD): What Are the Implications?" *International Dyslexia Association.*

Texas Council for Developmental Disabilities. 2013. "What Is a Developmental Disability?" www.tcdd.texas.gov/resources/what-is-developmental-disability/ (accessed March 10, 2016).

Thompson, S. 1996. "Nonverbal Learning Disorders." Retrieved January 12, 2016 from www.ldonline.org/article/6114/

Torgesen, J.K. 2002. "Empirical and Theoretical Support for Direct Diagnosis of Learning Disabilities by Assessment of Intrinsic Processing Weaknesses." In *Identification of Learning Disabilities: Research to Practice,* eds. R. Bradley, L. Danielson, and D.P. Hallahan, 565–613. Mahwah, NJ: Lawrence Erlbaum.

Turnbull, H.R., N. Huerta, M. Stowe, L. Weldon, and S. Schrandt. 2009. *The Individuals with Disabilities Education Act as Amended in 2004.* New York: Pearson.

Vaughn, S., and L.S. Fuchs. 2003. "Redefining Learning Disabilities as Inadequate Response to Instruction: The Promise and Potential Problems." *Learning Disabilities Research & Practice* 18, no. 3, pp. 137–46.

Vernon, M., and K. Miller. 2001. "Interpreting in Mental Health Settings: Issues and Concerns." *American Annals of the Deaf* 146, no. 5, pp. 429–34.

Wagner, R.K., J.K. Torgesen, C.A. Rashotte, and N.A. Pearson. 2010. *TOSREC: Test of Silent Reading Efficiency and Comprehension.* Pro-Ed.

Wechsler, D., and J.A. Naglieri. 2006. *WNV: Wechsler Nonverbal Scale of Ability.* Pearson Education.

Wiederholt, J.L., D.D. Hammill, and V.L. Brown. 2009. *Reading Observation Scale (ROS).* Austin, TX: Pro-Ed.

Wiederholt, J.L., and V.L. Brown. 2012. *Gray Oral Reading Test-Fifth Edition: Examiner's Record Booklet; Form-A.* Austin, TX: Pro-Ed.

Wilkinson, G.S., and G.J. Robertson. 2006. *WRAT 4: Wide Range Achievement Test; Professional Manual.* Psychological Assessment Resources, Incorporated.

Zabala, J. 2010. *The SETT Framework for Assistive Technology* [DVD]. Roseville, MN: Division of Special Education Policy, Minnesota Department of Education.

Index